The Joy of
Living Live

A Raw Food Journey

Zakhah

The information in this book is based on the training, personal experiences and research of the author. It is not intended to take the place of professional medical treatment and the reader is encouraged to seek the advice of a health professional. This book is not to be sold as medical text. The author and publisher are not responsible for any adverse effects or consequences resulting from the use of any of the suggestions, preparations, or procedures in this book.

Zakhah

Published by
Communicators Press
P.O. Box 26063, Washington DC 20001
(202) 797-8110

ISBN 0-9701134-7-1

"And the Lord will take away from thee all sickness..."
Deuteronomy 7:15

(...when we follow the universal laws governing health)

Dedication

This book is dedicated to the pioneers who started this journey with small steps that created a giant leap into a new consciousness before it became popular. They understood that making healthy dietary changes into a lifestyle is revolutionary. Without their vision, this project would not be in existence. Their love, dedication, contributions and sacrifices on this path have spearheaded the continuous elevation of this diet.

To my family, I pray that you experience excellent health and life more abundantly.

A special thank you to Ahtur Yatsiliel for spending those many long hours to produce this fabulous layout and for his continued support for this project. Also to Sar Eliashuv and his family for their great assistance and access to resources. To especially Dodah Zvenah and Ahk Onam for their wonderful editing skills.

I want to give thanks to everyone who assisted with this project: Prince Aharon and his family, Prince Gavriel and his family, Prince Immanuel and his family, Ahtur Rofeh Ahmadiyah, Ahtur Ammioz B. N. Immanuel, Cohane Abir, Cohen Hecumliel and his family (I'm coming home!), Dr. Llaila O. Afrika, Dr. Aris LaTham, The House of Mahneel, Djenaba (thanks for the photo), T'meed-el and Eranah, Dick Gregory and his family, Karyn Calabrese (you are inspiring), Annette Larkins, Tolentin Chan, Storm and Jinjee Talifero (I love your spirit), Lynda Carter, Amen Khum Ra, Artis Eugene Hinson, Sister Migdah B. Yehuda, Sister Bilgah B. Israel, Sister Kanunah B. Israel, Brother Elinatahn, Lillian Butler, Zachary Ramzey III, Sister Sheliyah E. Hoshea and to anyone who I may not have mentioned, I want you to know that I love and appreciate you!

The Joy

You haven't REALLY been RAW until you...

- ❖ Eat at least 5 different varieties of the same fruit or vegetable
- ❖ Try at least 20 new foods that you NEVER thought you would eat
- ❖ Soak and sprout your own nuts, seeds, grains and beans
- ❖ Plant and harvest food from your own garden
- ❖ Prepare a raw meal for others that is so good, they begin preparing that same meal for others
- ❖ Can eat a meal of just cherries or mangoes or avocados or _____ and feel perfectly satisfied
- ❖ Can drink a fresh green juice straight up with nothing added
- ❖ Can identify at least 3 edible plants on a nature walk
- ❖ Watch the sunrise from the top of a mountain
- ❖ Watch the sunset from the shore of a beach
- ❖ Spend a night outside under the stars
- ❖ Shop in an open air market in a foreign country
- ❖ Shop in a local farmer's market
- ❖ Walk barefoot in a field of grass
- ❖ Drink young coconut water straight from the coconut
- ❖ Peel and chop a stalk of sugar cane
- ❖ Swim in a natural lake
- ❖ Attend a raw food retreat
- ❖ Feel completely happy and at peace with the Creator, the creation, humanity and yourself
- ❖ Can do these things without FEAR
- ❖ Start GLOWING and everyone tells you so
- ❖ Amaze your doctor
- ❖ Out-live your doctor

Contents

My Own Raw Journey

I grew up in Maryland, in a typical African American family. My parents were born in the South; raised on farms, and adopted the diet from slavery. My father introduced me to chitlins (hog's intestines). I remember walking home from elementary school and smelling something horrible coming at me down the street. Shocked that the smell came from my house, I stormed up the steps, angry because my house was filled with people- including my relatives visiting from North Carolina-yet no one had investigated the broken toilet. To my horror, I discovered that the foul aroma did not come from the bathroom, it came from the kitchen. I chose to go hungry that night. On another occasion, they served cow's tongue, but I just could not eat something that could taste me back. My mom was a little more health-conscious because the teachings of Dick Gregory influenced her father. She placed limits on my lack of health-consciousness by making sure I ate all of my vegetables and hiding the junk food to prevent me from devouring the whole supply. As the child of two working parents, I frequently ate "t.v." dinners, microwave meals, and processed foods. On Fridays, my mother did not cook, so either my father fried fish or we ate at fast food restaurants. I loved to eat and some of my favorite foods included pre-packaged macaroni and cheese, chicken liver, barbecued ribs, popcorn, cake and pizza. I ate white sugar like I drank water. I lived for junk food. Consequently, I often experienced illnesses as a child. I had colds all of the time, emotional imbalances, infections and eczema. My vision began blurring as a teenager, but I refused to wear glasses because I was more self-conscious about how I looked than if I could see.

At the age of 16, my life changed. I watched my grandmother die of cancer. It was the first time that someone I was close to passed away. My aunt made transition a few years before of the same disease. My grandfather died a few months after my grandmother from a broken heart. I searched for answers. I absolutely refused to believe that a God who could make the sun, the ocean, and the stars allowed people to "just get" horrible diseases with no cause and no cure. One day the answer came. A young preacher named Reverend Ernest Tuck spoke to my church youth group about the connection between diet, health, and spirituality. I stopped eating all meat that day and began to study my African history before slavery in the Americas. My mother told me that I would have to make my own meals because she didn't know what to feed me. For my school lunch, I would pack sandwiches of lettuce, sandwich spread, and cheese; a piece of fruit and some form of junk food (I reasoned that there was no meat in a piece of cake). In my zealousness, I failed to educate myself on how to properly feed myself, so I soon became very malnourished. My teachers were really concerned and told me that I should at least go back to eating chicken and fish until I learn how to balance my diet. I very reluctantly ate some when I felt weak. When I went to college the following year, I met other vegetarians who taught me how to cook and eat.

My first introduction to the raw food lifestyle occurred at 19 years old while I was working in New York City one summer. An independent radio station announced a weekend raw food retreat at a scenic resort in the mountains near Woodstock. It was just what I needed because my soul suffocated from the smog and lifelessness of that concrete jungle. Being an adventurous person, I got the information, jumped on a bus and headed on my way. Upon arrival, that's when I saw him- the most beautiful brother I had ever seen in my life. He looked like he had stepped out of the sky. Of course, his live-in girlfriend who was with him felt the same way, but I realized that if this diet and lifestyle could help people look like that, I was all for it. I had an absolutely wonderful time at the retreat, but unfortunately, the food did not taste very good. I did, however, understand the spirit of what the healers were trying to communicate about living a holistic life and it stuck with me. After the retreat, I began to live a "spiritual" life. I continued as a vegetarian, exercised more frequently, did yoga, had my first colema (colon irrigation), and attended classes with different African-centered organizations.

Traveling to Israel and spending time at the Everlasting Life Health Clinic owned by the African Hebrew Israelite Community convinced me to pursue a live diet. The peaceful environment allowed me to learn about health, nutrition, and how to overcome the lies that we have been told all of our lives about what and how to eat. Adopting a living foods diet and lifestyle is the key to maintaining good health forever. The holistic physicians explained the unhealthy effects that cooked food has on our bodies and showed us some graphic photos from Dr. Jensen's Guide to Better Bowel Care. From that point forward, for me, it has been an epic battle of woman versus stomach on my raw food journey. What made things even more difficult was working in a health food store upon my return to the States where I had access to all the food I wanted. I ate constantly. This, of course led to more health issues.

Then I discovered fasting. I learned that fasting could strengthen my immune system, heal acute disorders such as skin eruptions and digestive problems, and would increase my willpower. My first experiences with fasting were very unsuccessful. I soon learned that I had no willpower whatsoever. It took three attempts before I finally went a whole day without eating anything. Since then I have fasted many times. I fast once a week for the past seven years and I have done prolonged fasts such as a three-week one-hundred-percent live food fast, a fourteen-day "master cleanse" (consuming only water with fresh lemon juice, cayenne pepper, and maple syrup), and a forty-day liquid fast. Each time I come off of a fast, I get physically, mentally, and spiritually stronger.

Today, my diet is in constant elevation. I am completely vegan and eat mostly raw foods. I love to experiment with different recipes and love it even more when others enjoy them. My vision is perfect, it is extremely rare when I get sick, and all of the ailments I suffered from as a child are gone. I am often inspired by the stories of our ancestors "supernatural" capabilities of walking on water, walking through fire without getting burned, and making time stand still. I know that if we adopt all of the principles of the living foods lifestyle that the Creator gave us when He made us in His image, that we can move far beyond the parameters that we have been taught to accept and eradicate all injustices from the planet.

A Case Study On Human Nutrition

But ye are come unto Mount Zion, and unto the city of the living God, the heavenly Jerusalem, and to an innumerable company of angels

Hebrews 12:22

There is a human health experiment that has been conducted for the past 37 years. This experiment removed a group of African Americans from the ills of America, (as prophesied in Deuteronomy 28:15-68), and placed them in a controlled environment in Israel, Northeast Africa to determine the effects on their health in adhering to the Biblical laws of diet and lifestyle. In addition, these residents of Israel have no weapons, no locks on doors, no perversion, no homelessness, no starvation, and no crime. The results are unprecedented.

The African Hebrew Israelites of Jerusalem are comprised of approximately 2,500 men, women and children residing in three development towns - Dimona, Arad, and Mitspe Ramon - in southern Israel. The community, whose base is known internationally as the "Village of Peace", has, over the past three decades, fashioned an exemplary lifestyle, known for its lack of social trauma and for fostering an atmosphere of intellectual development, resourcefulness and creativity. The objective of the Hebrew Israelites is to establish the long-awaited Kingdom of God (Yah) on earth to be a light unto all and to demonstrate the benefits of living according to the word of Yah. The vibrant culture of the Hebrew Israelites - high moral standards, communal lifestyle, vegan diet, redemptive enterprises based in the principles of preventive health care and holistic social evolvement, the return to keeping the law according to the Torah (the first five books of the Bible) - serve as a model for regenerative living. This model is being replicated in progressive development projects in Ghana, Benin, other parts of Africa and the world.

The African Hebrew Israelites of Jerusalem are not only the healthiest people in the African Diaspora, but evidence is beginning to emerge suggesting that they are indeed the healthiest collective group of humans on the planet today. The Ministry of Health of this community has reported that there has been one case of diabetes, two strokes, one heart attack, one cancer patient, no prostate cancer, no STDs (sexually transmitted diseases), no HIV or AIDS, and no teen or young adult obesity in over 30 years among those who formerly lived in America. Meherry Medical College in Nashville, Tennessee reported the eradication of high blood pressure within the Hebrew Israelite community. According to the U.S. Center for Disease Control (CDC), African-Americans rank number one in each of the above-mentioned diseases. Since 1967, there have been fewer than 30 deaths in this community of over 2000 residents.

This outstanding level of health and social well-being is attributed to the adoption of a lifestyle that is in harmony with the laws and instructions of the God of Israel as given in the Bible. In this "Village of Peace," it is mandatory for every adult to exercise 3 times a week for 30 minutes until sweating. It is prescribed to receive a full-body massage once a month. The entire community is vegan- no consumption of animals (including, of course, no fish and no chicken) or their by-products (no dairy, no eggs), and no chemicals, artificial additives or preservatives. They eat only fresh fruits and vegetables, nuts, grains, legumes, and seeds. There is no smoking or alcohol consumption- except for naturally fermented fruit-based wines produced within the community. The Hebrew Israelite adults observe at least three no-salt days, one raw food day, and one day of fasting every single week. Four times a year, during the change of seasons, the community prepares to elevate their diet. They observe a "Sugarless Week" where the only sweeteners consumed are maple syrup, date syrup and green stevia (a sweet herb); and a "Live Foods Week" where members of the community consume 80% to 100% raw foods and also cleanse their digestive systems.

The Hebrew Israelites operate several health-conscious and environmentally-conscious businesses: a natural integrated therapies health spa, an experimental organic farm, a natural birthing center where over 1,000 babies were born without drugs or artificial means, a natural fabric design house and clothing production facility producing clothes made from natural materials (cotton, linen, silk, and wool), several health food stores, tofu factories in Israel and Ghana, Soul Vegetarian- the largest vegan restaurant chain in the world with 13 restaurants in 4 countries (and still growing), and much more. The community has developed pioneering advancement in potable water provision, alternative energy generation, and agricultural production that demonstrate how humans can sustainably live in harmony with the natural environment. Their expertise is being sought by countries on the continent of Africa, as well as in other parts of the world.

Hailed by the Israeli media as "an Island of Sanity" and by the United States Congress as a "Miracle in the Desert," the Hebrew Israelites have been studied by various sociologists and heralded for "leaping thousands of years of social evolution."* A significant element in the community's great achievements is the continued emphasis on study, research, growth, and elevation in righteousness. Under the divine leadership of their spiritual leader Ben Ammi HaMasheak, the Hebrew Israelite community is transcending the adverse effects of a dehumanizing four-hundred year captivity in America to achieving world acclaim. Truly, to move a people from eating pig intestines and chicken gizzards to bean burgers and sea vegetables in less than 40 years is phenomenal. They currently eat "The Sacred Diet" that consists of raw and steamed foods and whole food supplements. There are some, however, who have stepped out on the water to consume all or mostly raw foods. Understanding the constraints of the currently polluted global ecosystem, the Hebrew Israelites, as a whole, are moving closer to adopting a living foods diet.

* Israel Gerber, The Heritage Seekers, Johnathan David Publishers, Middle Village, NY, 1977.

Raw and Living Foods

And Yah said, Behold, I have given you every herb bearing seed, which is upon the face of all the earth, and every tree, in the which is the fruit of a tree yielding seed; to you it shall be for meat.

Genesis 1:29

Living foods are defined as fruits, vegetables, nuts, grains, and seeds that still contain living enzymes. Raw foods include living foods, and are also some transitional foods that may have been cooked during their processing after harvesting from the living plant, but need no additional cooking before their consumption.

All living things have enzymes. Enzymes are life-force energy. They are necessary for digestion. Cooking at temperatures above 105 degrees Fahrenheit destroys enzymes. When the body consumes foods with no enzymes, it must use its own limited enzyme reserve. If these enzymes are used faster than they are replaced, aging occurs. The longer we continue to consume foods without the proper amount of living enzymes, the older we grow. The continued aging makes it increasingly difficult to make up for the enzymes we are not replenishing our bodies with because we are not consuming living foods. Over time, the body begins to deteriorate, causing wrinkles, lack of energy, memory loss, poor vision, graying hair, hair loss, loss of libido, weakened bones, etc. Eating a proper diet of 80% to 100% live foods alleviates this loss of enzymes. An apple, even after it is picked from the tree is still able to breathe, feel energy, and reproduce. Plant the seed of this apple and it will produce an apple tree. Plant the seed of a cooked apple and it will produce nothing. Take a raw carrot and hit it as hard as you can against your kitchen counter. Now cook a whole carrot and do the same thing. Which one do you want your bones to be made out of?

The human body is at least 80% water. So it makes sense that our diet should be at least 80% water in order to maintain this balance. Foods with a high water-content are called alkaline foods. Foods with a low water-content are known as acidic. The general rule to remember is that animal products, cooked foods, proteins and starches are acidic. Fresh fruits, raw vegetables, and sprouts are alkaline. All acids burn. When cooked foods enter the digestive system, the body coats it with mucous so the sensitive tissue in the digestive system is not damaged. This mucous inhibits the absorption of whatever enzymes and nutrients that remain after the cooking process. Again, continued consumption of nutrient and enzyme deficient foods leads to disease and decay within the body.

In order for a disease to live within the body, it must have a disease-friendly environment in which to exist. This is why a virus does not exist in the same way in the body of a raw foodist as it does in the body of a meat-eater. Disease loves for you to eat chicken and sugar, drink cow's milk, smoke cigarettes, and have negative thoughts. Our bodies are polluted with years of mucous, waste, and uric acid that feed parasites, bacteria, and worms (disease) first inherited from the poor diet of our parents. These ills are caused by our unhealthy lifestyle. Once you make the environmental conditions unfriendly for disease by eliminating these bad habits and adopting good habits such as eating living foods, drinking green juices, exercising, thinking positively, etc., then the disease has no choice but to weaken and die. And you live.

Some who have decided to become vegans and raw foodists believe that achieving good health is solely based on what they eat. It is important to adhere to the nutritional principles of food combining, balance in the diet, consuming a variety of fresh organic foods, whole food supplementation, exercise, and detoxifying the body. The lack of understanding of these principles could lead to bone and tooth loss, malnutrition, brain deficiencies, poor digestion, and much more. Many have changed their diets because they experienced poor health when consuming their former diet of meat, sugar, starch and salt. Unfortunately, if poor nutritional behaviors were practiced when eating a cooked diet, repeating those same poor behaviors while consuming a raw food diet will not heal the body. Good health is a holistic process that requires a total positive change in mentality, a well-balanced diet and good habits. **It does not make sense to be a meat-eating animal activist, alcoholic vegetarian, obese vegan, smoking raw-foodist, or a cursing breathatarian.** Change doesn't happen overnight because habits do not develop overnight.

Transitioning into the living foods lifestyle may initially cause you to experience changes in health, body weight and energy level as your body is breaking down your cooked cells and replacing them with vibrant live cells. Live foods maintain more of their vitamin and mineral content than cooked food, so over time you may not eat as much. In the beginning, you may want to include some of your favorite cooked foods in your diet, but over time you may lose the taste for these things and gain a new taste for raw and living foods. Initially, you may live in a polluted urban environment, but as you do more research and your cellular composition changes, you may desire to move to a more natural and cleaner environment. You will need assistance from a holistic physician with eliminating toxins from your body. Pay close attention to what happens to your body.

This book is meant to be used as a tool to transition from the cooked food diet to the living foods diet. It must be supplemented with certain "superfoods" (see page **17**) in order to be effective. Some recipes include raw and cooked products as one is adjusting to a temperature change and texture of living foods. Each recipe can be adjusted to eliminate the salt, sugar, and cooked products as you elevate higher. The best way to eat is to consume one type of food at a time, but moving to a live foods diet is a process and we are all at different levels of development. Move at a pace that is comfortable for you as you continously strive to elevate your lifestyle.

Making The Right Transition

A live diet is ideal in that raw foods enhance physical and spiritual regeneration. A live diet should be the ultimate goal of all who seek this enhancement on the path to life everlasting. It is a return to the Genesis idea, the original diet which was given to man in Genesis 1:29. Today, however, because of the physical and spiritual transformations that man has undergone as a result of his own worldly programs, there most definitely *has to be* a transitioning period on the path of return, purging out the old to make way for the new.

There are several keys to transitioning. Maintain balance in all things (example: no "crash dieting", such as all fruit or all liquids, etc.) We are working towards holistic changes in lifestyle that will ensure permanent and positive results. Begin with a cleansing program. Maintain an exercise program. Strive to maintain regular bowel movements, more than once daily. In the beginning once daily may be an accomplishment if this has not been the case.

Include in your daily consumption a variety of what is in season of fruits and vegetables. Nuts, seeds, and grains should also be a part of the daily diet. At this stage of our development in the Hebrew Israelite Community, we do use soy products on the live program. Soybeans contain 35 to 40% more protein than meat, fish, eggs and cheese. We do no further cooking of the tofu. We use grains that can be soaked and eaten without further cooking, specifically bulgur and buckwheat. Include a variety of sea vegetables regularly, especially kelp and hijiki on a daily basis. DO NOT LEAVE OUT THE 7 DAILY RECOMMENDED SUPPLEMENTS: blackstrap molasses, fenugreek powder, kelp, wheat germ, brewer's yeast, parsley, and sesame seeds (see following page). Consume organic sprouts in your diet on a daily basis. Sprouts can be the base of the salad two to three times weekly.

WE RECOMMEND THIS TRANSITION TO A LIVE DIET BE UNDERTAKEN ONLY UNDER THE SUPERVISION OF YOUR HEALTHCARE PROVIDER, KEEPING YOUR HEALTHCARE PROVIDER ABREAST OF ALL DEVELOPMENTS. This should initially take place at least every three months or whenever something occurs, positive or negative. Initially, a physical examination is recommended, inclusive of a complete blood check. The blood work should be repeated in three months, then again in six months, and thereafter as recommended by the healthcare provider. This is to monitor and offset any physical situations that could occur due to change in diet.

Dr. Ahturah Karaliah E. N. Gavriel
Ministry of Divine Health
African Hebrew Isralites of Jerusalem

Seven Daily Whole Food Supplements

Supplement your raw diet with these "superfoods" for a complete nutritional experience. These amounts are for older children and adults. For quantities for infants and young children, see The Sacred Diet by Rofah Karaliah E. Nasik Gavriel (Communicators Press). This book contains easy ways to incorporate these essential foods into your diet.

Blackstrap Molasses- This is a rich source of vitamins and minerals. It is the residue of the last possible extraction of sugar from the cane or the beet. Molasses contains more calcium than milk, more iron than eggs and more potassium than any food, and is an excellent source of B vitamins (including B-12). It is also rich in copper, magnesium, phosporous, pantothenic acid, inositol and vitamin E. It is a good source of natural sugars. Mix one tablespoon of molasses in one cup of water and drink once a day.

Sesame Seeds – These are rich in protein; the B complex vitamins, vitamins A, D, and E; phosphorous, calcuim, iron, potassium, magnesium, zinc and unsaturated fatty acids. Sesame seeds are high in calcium and contain valuable enzymes. Consume a 1/2 cup of ground seeds daily. Sprouted seeds may be consumed.

Kelp- Kelp is one of the best sources of iodine. It is also rich in B-complex vitamins, vitamin D, E, and K, calcium and magnesium. Consume one tablespoon each day.

Brewers Yeast- This is a non-leavening yeast that can be added to all foods to increase their nutritional value. It is one of the best known vegetarian sources of the B vitamins, especially B-12. It contains 16 amino acids (proteins), 14 minerals and 17 vitamins. Consume at least one tablespoon with meals.

Fresh Parsley- Parsley contains more vitamin A per ounce than carrots, three times as much vitamin C as oranges and twice as much iron as spinach. Consume ¼ cup (3 sprigs) every day.

Fenugreek - This herb is 22% protein, contains an abundance of vitamins and minerals, especially the B vitamins, iron, all essential amino acids and natural quinine. Fenugreek does wonders for the sick and /or debilitated. It is a great preventive measure against illness in babies, children, and adults. Stir 1 to 2 tablespoons of powder in 1 cup of water and soak overnight. Drink water off the top and discard pulp. Sprouted seeds may be consumed.

Wheatgerm- This is the heart of the kernel of wheat. It is an excellent source of protein (24 grams per ½ cup), B complex vitamins, one of the richest known sources of vitamin E, and iron. It also contains copper, magnesium, manganese, calcium, phosphorous and is high in unsaturated fatty acids. Consume 6 tablespoons every day. This may cause many raw foodists to cringe, but consume the toasted variety because it increases the level of zinc.

Exercise!

"Running or fast walking builds up the heat in your body. When you finish, the body cools itself down. This process kills bacteria. No bacteria can live in this environment. We, [the Hebrew Israelites of Jerusalem] are to be the first on the planet who resist disease, sickness and death."

Ben Ammi HaMasheak, 2004 Unity Day Run in Dimona, Israel

Exercise is very important in the Hebrew Israelite Community. The Health Sanctuary, our health center, offers classes for expectant mothers, injury rehabilitation, group and private classes, positive energy touch therapy (better than a massage), reflexology and iridology. The Art of Divine Life Discipline, the name given to our cultural exercises, is a combination of breathing, stretching, free weights, cardiovascular activities, arts of peace (martial arts), running, swimming, jumping rope, yoga, high-low-or –no impact aerobics, etc. The name itself indicates the goal of the activities: (1) divine- pleasing unto God, (2) life- we don't believe in death, (3) and discipline- order, limits, and parameters. We connect these activities to lifestyles of righteousness. We cannot disconnect exercises from diet, dress, language, culture and lifestyle. On the surface, our exercises may look like those of other cultures, but the difference is that there is a marked improvement in the conditions of our people. In other cultures, there are people who do great exercises, then eat a pizza or fast food. In our culture, we have women over 40 who have healthy babies born at our natural birthing center and over 1000 babies born to parents who practice the lifestyle. The environment has to be holistic.

"Exercise is important. Many worry about how they can fit it into their life. Exercise is Life."

We call ourselves "human beings" when we are actually "human doings." You have to actively **do** something right each and every day in order to live. We cannot ascribe to higher forms of life without discipline. If you have discipline and share the technique with others, you are more powerful. Great people displayed discipline and that's what made them great. The five elements of life are attitude, diet, exercise, rest and relaxation, and proper elimination. When you are 50 years old, you are supposed to have more value and worth. Remember in the Scriptures that a 600 year old man built the Ark, not a 20 year old. It's a Greco-Roman concept to promote the image of physical strength as determined by the size of one's muscles or how much weight a person can lift. Most of these athletes die young from heart attacks caused by the abnormal muscle development putting stress on the heart.

Be firm in your purpose for eating raw food. Everything begins with a thought. Keep thinking it; it will happen. The body renews itself every 7 years. The goal is to regenerate cells that are not degenerating because the degenerate cell will lead to death. Each time you breathe, you should be breathing in life energy so you don't get sick, so you don't experience a physical death. The process is to slow down death, stop it, and then reverse it. We have to live long enough to forget the former things as mentioned in Revelations 21:1-8. We have to forget about doing the things that were killing us because focusing on those thoughts will only bring us more death. We have to energize only life-giving thoughts if we want to live forever. Life is a sacred experience. What can be more holy than preserving the vessels of the image of Yah. This vessel was meant to be eternal.

Abir HaCohen
Divine Ministry of Edenic Exercise
African Hebrew Israelites of Jerusalem

Eat Organic!

Man was made from the minerals of the earth. A decline in minerals equals a decline in health, leading to death. The Hebrew Israelites practice what is termed Divine Agriculture, a non-animal-based agricultural system inspired by Genesis 2:15. The law is to keep and till the earth so that the earth can yield its strength. The land is kept according to scriptural law: (1) there is no sowing/mixing of diverse seeds; (2) the land rests every seven years; (3) there are no animals in the field; and (4) the land must be sanctified. We do not use the fertilizers permitted in "organic" farming such as ground fish bones and dried cows blood. We do use cow manure as compost.

We operate four and one-half acres of experimental farm land certified by the State of Israel. We produce vegetables that cleanse and rebuild cells. These include brassica (cancer-fighting) produce such as broccoli, kale, cauliflower, mustard greens and turnips; and also blood-builders such as beets and spinach. Our charge is the change our DNA from a malnourished inferior state, to a highly-mineralized and divine state. For the past 15 years, we have been producing with great results. Our food has been tested over the years. Our broccoli has always had more minerals than commercial broccoli and 50% more minerals than other organic broccoli. Our watermelons are heavier in weight, meaning the mineral content is greater. The phenomena of the year we had an over-abundant squash crop was the birth of an exceptional number of sets of twins per capita being born in our community.

It is dangerous to eat food treated with pesticides. The chemical process is based on salt-based dehydration of plants. Pesticides have to be water soluble so the dehydrated plant can drink them. The chemicals then bind with the cells of the plant. When we eat the plants treated with the pesticides, the chemicals bind with the blood in the body, depleting the body of nutrients and oxygen. For example, "Blue baby" syndrome, a rare and sometimes fatal disease, is caused by chemicals from the mother's diet getting into the baby's bloodstream, blocking the oxygenation causing the baby to suffocate internally. There are no pesticides that are non-mutative. If you eat it, then you become something else. They can not be washed off because they are inside the food. It is still important to wash* produce because the pathogens from the food handlers get in the air and on the food potentially spreading hepatitis, meningitis, and jaundice. If you don't grow your own food, then it's best to go to backyard organic farmers. Whatever the price is, it's worth it. It's not about the food you eat, but the quality.

Elinatahn Ben Israel
Ministry of Divine Agriculture, African Hebrew Israelites of Jerusalem

* Wash produce with salt or a natural vegetable wash because the chemicals in detergent soaps combined with the chemical pesticides can result in a toxic chemical reaction in the body.

Prayer & Meditation

Effective Prayer

All great events involving the truly conscious are preceded by prayer. Prayers are petitions, supplications, praises, and thanksgiving made unto the Creator. For our prayers to be effective and bring forth the promised effects, we must first know if the Creator is with us and if He is hearing our prayers.

In the liberal democratic Christian societies, we are taught that we can eat anything as long as we pray over it. African Edenic people the world over are paying the horrendous price, (heart disease, obesity, diabetes, cancers, high blood pressure, sickness, plagues and death), for believing these diabolical lies. This is an example of prayers not being effective. Their prayers cannot change the truth of dietary consciousness, and cannot halt the onslaught of the lethal diseases that result from the consumption of swine, mad cow, mercury fish, and high-fat, fried, processed, chemical, denatured junk foods.

Divine Meditation

In this new age of supposed enlightenment, meditation has come to mean that one must empty the mind entirely of all conceptual thought and let the spirit abide in emptiness, silence and stillness. Only in that state will the spirit fully awaken to seek long lost unity with the void and grasp the truth of the universe. **These beliefs are in direct contradiction with the ancient African Hebraic wisdom which is recorded in the Holy Scriptures.**

> *"This book of the law shall not depart out of your mouth but you shall meditate therein day and night, that you may observe to do according to all that is written therein for then you shall make your way prosperous and then you shall have good success"*

> ***Joshua 1:8***

We are familiar with the saying "an idle mind is the devil's workshop." When you meditate on nothing, your mind is idle and open to be infiltrated by adversarial doctrine. Therefore, we advocate a form of meditation in which you vocalize and contemplate and speak the laws, instructions, and principles of the Creator day and night. This kind of meditation causes these thoughts concepts and words (the Holy Spirit) to be energized and brought into realization leading us to prosperity and success according to universal law.

Hecumliel HaCohen
Divine Prophetic Priesthood, African Hebrew Israelites of Jerusalem

The Benefits of Fasting

Fasting is the abstention of an activity- in this case, eating. It aids the body in purification by removing toxins, clearing dead cells, and rejuvenating and rebalancing the body. It allows clarity of mind so one can focus on and elevate thought and activity. Fasting is a guaranteed and healthy way to lose weight. This process also has been shown to alleviate many diseases such as allergies, constipation, and asthma. Studies done at fasting clinics in Europe have shown that under proper supervision a person can fast for 40 days on water and 100 days on juices with no danger.

The mere discussion of going without food causes fear in people because of our conditioned thinking. Studies have shown, however, that more diseases are caused by overeating than undereating. The digestion process requires a significant amount of energy. For example, after the completion of a large cooked meal, one may feel sleepy. It takes energy away from the immune system and other functions of the body.

Some believe that sleeping is sufficient for the regeneration process of the body. Sleeping is indeed a small-scale fast that cleanses the body and allows it to heal from some of the daily stresses that we place upon it. Unfortunately, most Americans do not get enough sleep to complete the cleansing and healing process.

Fasting is a more intensive process. After the second or third day of the fast, the body goes into a process called "autolysis" where it begins to digest its own cells. The body selectively eliminates cells and tissue that are in excess, diseased, damaged, aged, or dead. After three days, the body expels toxins and cleanses the blood. In five days the process of healing and rebuilding the immune system begins. After a ten-day fast, potential future diseases are eradicated before they even develop. When autolysis takes place, the healthiest living cells remain.

There are several types of fasts. For those fasting for the first time, it is advised that one consume a variety of raw or uncooked fruits and vegetables, and drink water and juice for one day. This fast can be repeated in a defined cycle such as once a week or during the change in seasons. A single fast is not as effective as repeated fast. As one becomes more advanced, one can try a juice fast, drinking only fresh-squeezed juices. These juices are not from concentrate or pasteurized because these processes kill the living enzymes needed for energy. Be sure to drink eight glasses of water daily when on this type of fast to prevent dehydration. A water fast is for those with experience because it releases toxins so quickly that it can cause an individual to become sick. This sickness is called a "healing crisis"- a process that occurs because the body must eliminate the older, weaker cells before rebuilding itself.

Man was made in the image and likeness of God, as stated in Genesis. In this Genesis Cycle, God worked for 6 days and rested on the seventh. In this image that complete cycle of rest, would include the abstention of eating. If the greatest consciousness in the universe, He who created us in His image can take a break, then why can't we?

"The human body was not designed to eat every single day."

Traditional farming practices involve cultivating the land for six years, and then allowing the land to rest during the seventh year. This allows the land to rejuvenate and continue to bring forth life. Likewise, if the human body rests by abstaining from food, work, etc., one day per week, then after one year, it has rested for 52 days. After seven years, the body has rested for one year or 364 days. Every seven years, the body is recreated with new cells. A person is literally transformed.

We should also take note of some precautions with fasting. Pregnant and lactating women should never fast. It is unhealthy for people who are more than 10 pounds underweight to fast. Diabetics and those with severe hypoglycemia should only fast under medical supervision. In addition, people with severe wasting diseases such as neurological degenerative diseases like Alzheimer's disease will generally not benefit from fasting. (As a side note: these diseases can be transmitted by eating the flesh of animals infected with chronic wasting diseases.)

After completing a fast, it is a great time to improve eating habits in order to reap the benefits of this healing process. The body is a temple that houses the spirit of the Creator. We must begin to treat it as such. Only then can we begin to tap into those higher spiritual powers. Can you image the possibilities in the different areas of our lives? The original plan is for man to exist on the earth as a young and beautiful being forever. This is everlasting life. Fasting is one of the keys to the eternal fountain of youth.

Why Sprout?

Sprouting is an essential component of the raw food diet. Many of us vegans and raw foodists are eating denatured foods- unsprouted seeds and beans, unsoaked nuts, pesticide-laden-genetically-engineered fruits and vegetables, cooked (pasteurized) juices, and stagnant (bottled, spring, distilled) water because these things are fast and affordable. Sprouts may not be a fast food, but they are definitely a very inexpensive way to gain massive amounts of nutrients. They are rich in vitamins A, B, and C. Sprouts are one of the greatest sources of complete and digestible protein.

	Calcium	Iron	Protein	Vitamin C	Vitamin B-6
Lentils, Sprouted, Raw (100g)	25 mg	3.21 mg	8.96 g	16.5 mg	0.190 mg
Lentils, cooked (100g)	19 mg	3.3 mg	9.02 g	1.5 mg	0.178 mg

Source: U.S. Department of Agriculture National Nutrient Database

Sprouted nuts, seeds, and beans seem to have a similar vitamin and mineral content as their cooked counterparts. What distinguishes sprouts is that their nutrients are in a bio-available form that the body can easily digest. For example, if you were to eat dry raw lentils, your body could not extract its nutrients and they will simply come out of you looking exactly the same, but giving you gas and indigestion along the way. This is due to the foods' natural security system called enzyme inhibitors. These enzyme inhibitors cause the living energy of these foods to lie dormant until the foods are ready to be planted or reproduce. A bean can be stored in a cool dry place for years and still sprout after coming in contact with water.

When you eat cooked lentils, as most of us do, you can extract more due to the water content, but your body would still be starved for nutrients because the cooking changes the structure of the lentils into a form unrecognized by the body. This contributes to such illnesses as obesity. Whenever fire is added to something, it changes form. If you sprout the raw lentils, the percentage of nutrients that your body is able to absorb greatly increases. This concept is only recently understood by the nutrition world, so there are not many extensive studies on this process. Despite the scientific data. It is easy to tell the difference in how you feel after you consume a cup of cooked beans versus a cup of raw bean sprouts.

Many seeds sold at commercial stores are treated so they will not germinate. To obtain seeds for sprouting, purchase them from an independent source such as the two listed below:

The Sproutpeople 225 Main Street, Gays Mills, WI 54631. Phone: 1-877-777-6887. www.sproutpeople.com
The Sprout Man, P.O. Box 1100, Great Barrington MA 01230. Phone: (413) 528-5200. www.sproutman.com

How to Sprout

Sprouting is very easy. It is best to grow your own sprouts because it is less expensive and you control the temperature and sanitary conditions. You can sprout seeds like flax, fenugreek, pumpkin, sunflower, alfalfa; beans, including soy and garbanzo (chickpeas), grasses such as wild rice; grains, among them are wheat, kamut, quinoa; and herbs such as anise star and red clover.

Materials for sprouting include:

Nuts, grains, seeds or beans of your choice
Sprout jar with an opening wide enough to fit your hand
Cheesecloth or screen
Rubber band
Water

1. Rinse a cup of your desired seeds to remove rocks and debris. Remove broken or discolored seeds. Place them in a glass jar and cover with two cups of purified water. Cover the top of the jar with cheesecloth and secure with a rubber band.

2. Soak your seeds according to the chart on the following page.

3. In the morning, leaving the cheesecloth covering in place, drain the contents of the jar.

4. Lie the jar on its side in a location that is warm and away from direct sunlight.

5. Rinse the jar's contents through the screen as many times as indicated to prevent the formation of mold and fungus. For example, for 2 rinses, rinse once in the morning and once in the evening.

6. After a day or two, you may begin to see a small growth appear. You may begin to use them at this point or allow it to grow for a few days. (See chart on next page.) Sprouts can be refrigerated for up to three days. Do not refrigerate wet sprouts.

Sprouting Chart

Plant Type	Quantity	Yield (cups)	Sprout Length (inches)	Soaking Hours	Rinses Per Day	Days to Sprout
Alfalfa	3 Tbsp	3	1-2	4-6	4	4
Most Beans	1 cup	3-4	1	8-10	3	4
Barley	½ cup	1	0	8-10	3	3
Buckwheat	1 cup	2-3	½	4-6	2	3
Chickpeas	1 cup	3	½	10-12	3	3
Flax Seeds *	1 Tbsp	1	1-2	5-7	5	4
Fenugreek	1 Tbsp	1	2-3	4-6	4	4
Lentils	1 cup	2	¼ - ½	6-8	3	4
Millet *	1 cup	1 ½	0- 1/8	6-8	3	4
Mung Beans	1 cup	3-4	1-2	8-10	2	5
Mustard	1 Tbsp	1	1 ½	4-6	2	4
Most Nuts	1 cup	1 ½	0	8-12	2	1
Onion	1 Tbsp	1	1-2	4-6	2	4
Oats	1 cup	2	0 – ¼	8-10	2	3
Pumpkin Seeds	1 cup	1 ½	0 -1/8	6-8	3	2
Sesame Seeds	1 cup	1 ½	0	4-6	4	1
Sunflower	1 cup	1 ½	0 – 1/8	6-8	2	2
Soybeans	1 cup	2 ½	½ - 1	10-12	5	4
Rice **	1 cup	1 ½	0 – 1/8	8-10	4	3
Quinoa*	1 cup	2 ½	0- 1/16	4-6	3	3
Wheat	1 cup	1 ½	0 – 1/8	10-12	4	3

* Sprout on a screen or in a sprout bag because seeds will be very soft. Flax seeds become gelatinous. Just sprinkle on water instead of rinsing.

** Wild rice and whole-grain brown rice only.

Detoxification

Cleaning the inside of the body is just as important as the food that goes into it. It is essential to the maintenance of good health. Our digestive systems are not like a baby's where we eat and 30 minutes later we eliminate. An adult colon or large intestines is about five feet long and yours may holding ten to well over twenty-five pounds of fecal matter. When we consume cooked food, the colon creates mucous to coat it as it goes through the intestines. Inside the large intestines, water is drawn out of this matter and a sticky plaque remains which hardens on the intestinal walls. What is worse is that waste can be impacted in "pockets" in the intestines and over time a layer of tissue forms over the pocket, sealing in the waste which will continue to poison the body.

Waste particles back up into our circulatory system. The blood flows throughout the body carrying the waste along with it. For example, when waste builds up in our heart, it leads to heart attacks and strokes. When it builds up in our brain, it literally destroys our minds. The body attempts to slow the destruction of our major organs by pushing the waste out of our largest eliminatory organ- the skin. This can result in acne, eczema, rashes, running sores, and more.

Cleansing the colon causes this process to reverse itself. The colon eliminates waste and opens intestinal pockets. The blood gradually carries waste from the organs back to the colon so the cells have a chance to strengthen and rebuild themselves, and skin problems clear up. Nobel Prize winner Dr. Alexis Carrel artificially kept a chicken heart alive in his laboratory for 38 years by bathing it in clean water to remove waste products. The heart died only after his assistant forgot to change the water, but Dr. Carrel concluded that cells could live indefinitely and that the key to life is to feed nutrients to cells, to remove toxins from the cells and to saturate the cells with oxygen. If cells do not receive nutrients and toxins are not removed, then the cells will be poisoned by their own waste.

There are many cleansing methods available. **Prune juice** is high in fiber and assists the liver in cleaning toxins from the body. **Aloe Vera Juice** regulates bowel movements. **Psyllium husk** coats the intestines and facilitates bowel movements. Drink lots of water when consuming. Works extremely well with aloe vera gel or juice. **Garlic and olive oil** kills parasites and strengthens the immune system. **Senna leaf tea** is an herbal laxative. **Enemas** are self-administered cleansing methods for the base of the colon. **Colon hydrotherapy** includes colonics and colemas which use water to massage and deeply cleanse the colon to remove years of impacted waste.

It is important to clean out at least every 3 months during the change in seasons and sisters should clean out once a month the week before their cycle begins. Too much detoxifying destroys the natural good bacteria. Not enough good bacteria leads to illness. In addition, stay in contact with a holistic physcian because any known or unknown illness that has been suppressed inside your body in the past may appear as your body detoxifies. Detoxifying along with a living foods lifestyle literally puts a new body in place while the old one fades away.

20 Simple Things to Improve Your Health

1. **Stop Eating Meat**. Organic, free-range, red, white, "the other white", or otherwise. They are all poisonous. You are what you eat. So if you eat a dead animal, then guess what? Consuming dead meat can only produce dead cells, dead thoughts, and a dead attitude in this death-oriented society. When you are dead, your service to the living Creations is over. We have to return to the cycle life if we want to live forever.

2. **Don't Drink Milk**. Ninety-nine percent of people of color are lactose intolerant. They lack the gene necessary to digest the primary milk sugar called lactose. This gene is found in baby cows. In addition to calcium, one glass of cow's milk contains puss cells, mucous, blood, live bacteria, hormones, and toxins that trigger diseases, such as asthma and diabetes, in humans. The promotion of cow's milk to our people is biological warfare. Drink vitamin-rich soy, seed, and nut milks and dark green leafy vegetable juices instead.

3. **Reduce Sugar**. It's more addictive than crack cocaine, but its legal. Sugar goes by the aliases of "brown sugar," "cane sugar," "cane juice," "corn syrup," "brown rice syrup," "fructose," "lactose," "sucrose," "fruit juice concentrate" and more. It leads to tooth decay, depletes the body of vital nutrients, and wears down the immune system. We consume it like oxygen in almost everything we eat. Replace sugar with any of the natural sweeteners listed on pages **40** to **41**. Eat naturally sweet uncooked fruit as a separate meal. Another option is curbing your sugar craving by drinking Sesame Seed Milk (see recipe on page **52**). Also balance your diet with dark green leafy vegetables and natural "good" (unsaturated fat which lowers cholesterol) fatty foods such as avocados and flax seed oil.

4. **Avoid Drinking and Eating at the Same Time**. Liquids dilute the digestive juices in your stomach so your body is unable to properly process the food. Again, this is another stressful, disease-causing habit we need to break. It is better to drink 30 minutes before eating or 2 hours after eating.

5. **Drink Water**. At least 8 glasses a day. The initial cause of most diseases is chronic dehydration. The body is over eighty-percent water. So guess what? Most of our diet should consist of the same thing (drinking water and water from fresh juices and raw fruits and vegetables). Drinking water clears and softens the skin, helps the body to eliminate toxins and waste, provides energy, enables the blood to flow, the brain to think, the muscles to stretch. All of our bodily systems are tied into the use of water. Avoid tap water, and try

a variety of bottled and filtered waters. Squeeze in a fresh lemon to add minerals, for a different taste and as a blood cleanser.

6. **Chew Your Food** twenty-five times before swallowing. Your mouth is the only place you can chew your food. We place too much stress on our stomachs by rushing and gulping down food. Constant improper eating wears out the digestive system, leading to disorders such as indigestion, constipation, gas, and, ultimately, chronic diseases such as colon cancer. Try this: Sit down, calm down, and enjoy your food. You deserve it!

7. **Eat a Salad** with each meal except when eating fruit. The living enzymes in a salad act as a broom to sweep the colon of the many starchy foods that have stuck to and hardened on the walls of the intestines. See Dr. Jensen's Guide to Better Bowel Care (Avery Books) for photographs. A fresh salad balances a "well-balanced" meal. In addition to the lettuce, tomatoes, and carrots, add some artichokes, black olives, avocados (natural "good" fat), seaweed, and seasonings to make your salad tasty and fun.

8. **An Apple A Day…** Eat five to nine raw fruits and vegetables each day. Eating living foods gives our bodies life and energy to handle the daily stresses of life. Cancer cells cannot live on the natural enzymes of living foods. All vitamins and minerals can be acquired from a variety of uncooked fruits, vegetables, nuts, seeds, and sprouted grains. No, this doesn't mean that you are limited to apples and carrots. Keep reading to find creative and exciting raw food recipes.

9. **Eat Sea Vegetables**. They have trace minerals that cannot be acquired from our daily diet. It fights energy-draining and cancer-causing radiation from the constant exposure to cell phones, computers, radios, etc. There is a wide variety of tastes and textures of seaweed. Kelp provides calcium and is a good salt substitute. Dulse prevents gray hair. Spirulina provides protein and curbs your appetite. Nori wraps are a healthier way of eating a sandwich without the bread. There are many types of seaweed snacks that can replace potato chips. Visit your local health food store or Asian Market to see the many choices available.

10. **Eat Natural Food Supplements**. Let's face it. We have heard the reports. The soil has been depleted of nutrients, so we are still not receiving sufficient amounts of vitamins and minerals from our food. This does not mean that we have to pop expensive vitamins supplements all day. Instead, we can get additional nutrients from these "super foods": brewer's yeast (vitamin B complex), blackstrap molasses (iron and calcium), parsley (vitamins A and C), fenugreek ("cure-all"), sesame seeds (calcium and phosphorus), kelp (calcium),

sprouted beans nuts and seeds (protein, vitamins B and C) and wheat germ (vitamin E and iron). For more details on how to add these foods to your diet, see page **17**.

11. **Fast**. Despite popular belief, the body was not designed to eat every single day. Americans suffer from far more diseases caused by overeating than by undereating. Fasting is the abstention of food. Fasting cleanses your blood, clarifies thinking, strengthens your internal organs, strengthens the immune system, regulates all bodily systems, pushes toxins out of the body, and (when done properly) is a guaranteed method of weight loss. Give your stomach a break. Spend a day once a week just drinking liquids (water and fresh-squeezed juices). You may think that you are too busy to do this, but nobody benefits from you wearing yourself down- except for your doctor.

12. **Break the Television Addiction**. It's a waste of time and energy. Studies show that people who watch television are more overweight and out of shape than those who do not. Try doing something else. Read a book. Spark conversation. Exercise. Go to a museum or to the park. Enroll in a class that teaches you something that you have always wanted to learn. Life is what you make it. Live your life instead of watching others live theirs on television.

13. **Be Careful and Pay Attention**. According to the Center for Disease Control, one of the ten leading causes of death and injury in the U.S. is accidents- primarily, car accidents. Oftentimes, we become involved in accidents when we are sleepy which causes our attention to get diverted or our nerves to be on edge. True, some accidents are unavoidable, but in most cases we can control the situation. Take your time, relax, focus, plan, learn when and how to say "No," read the instructions, listen to instructions, listen to that voice inside your head (common sense)- all of these things could save your life one day. Everything happens when its supposed to happen and the world will not stop spinning if you stop rushing.

14. **Exercise** three times a week for 30 minutes until you sweat. You can walk, run, swim, bike, hike, dance- whatever your schedule allows. It increases your heart rate which causes blood vessels to expand, preventing clogged arteries and enabling oxygen to reach your vital organs. You will become more energetic, intelligent, and vibrant. Make time. Your life depends on it.

15. **Stretch**. Keeping your body elastic helps to keep you looking younger longer. Do it in the morning after getting out of bed. It warms up the muscles before exercising to prevent muscle strain and tearing. Stretching after exercise or frequently after repetitive motions prevents muscle cramping and stiffness. Remember to drink plenty of water.

16. **Get Enough Sleep**. You need five to eight hours per night depending on your diet and lifestyle. During sleep, your breathing becomes regulated so enough oxygen gets to your vital organs and cleanses your blood. Your immune system gets stronger so you can fight disease. Your cells repair themselves and heal the body. The mind can relax and send you messages to assist you in your life journey via dreams.

17. **Breathe**. Inhale, pushing the stomach out. Exhale, pulling the stomach in. Take a few minutes to try it. It is impossible to feel upset when breathing this way. Breath is the key to life. When we are babies, this is how we automatically breathe. Star athletes and singers are taught to properly breathe to enhance performance. It allows sufficient oxygen to get to the brain and improves circulation. So, why wait to exhale? You can do it right now.

18. **Let It Go**. Whatever it is that is preventing you from enjoying the beauty of life. Free yourself from the pain, the anger, the hurt, the disappointment. Whoever did it, forgive them and move on with your life. Talk it out; scream it out; write it out; pray it out. Whatever you have to do, don't hold on it. Why would you want to keep it anyway? Those feelings and emotions physically settle in our heart, then we wonder why our heart attacks us. Happy people are healthier. There is a direct correlation between happiness and a stronger immune system: positivity (+) adds to your life and negativity (-) takes it away.

19. **Meditate**. Nothing complicated. It can be as simple as taking 5 minutes in the morning & 5 minutes before bed to reflect on your day. What do you want to accomplish and what have you learned? It is important to keep the focus on your life purpose so you are not consumed by the daily stresses of life. Ask the Creator what He wants of you. Open yourself up to listen for the answer (via thoughts or people). Design a plan for how to stay aligned with your purpose and the Universe will open up to help you. Obstacles exist only to test how serious you are about serving. Learn to divinely use your current situation and resources to accomplish the goal.

20. **Pray**. Science says praying causes positive chemical changes to occur in your body. Submitting to a higher power helps you to regain your focus. Find a quiet place. Thank the Creator for your blessings. Say what you will do for Him (and mean it). Ask for what you want, and then get up off your knees and make it happen. You will be surprised at the difference it will make in your day.

Holistic Dental Care

One of the side effects of a living diet is that you may experience an increase in your level of joy. This may include smiling, so it is important to take care of yours. Most cavities are caused by poor nutrition and poor oral hygiene. Here are some points to keep in mind while elevating your diet, so your teeth also experience a long healthy life.

- An overly acidic diet includes fried, sugary, and starchy foods and lacks adequate fresh raw whole fruits and vegetables. This diet creates an acidic condition in the body that contributes to tooth decay. Even on the raw diet, we may have a tendancy to <u>over</u>-consume nuts, seeds, sweet fruits, and citrus fruits. Balance your diet with dark green leafy vegetables, sprouts, and non-sweet fruits (any food with a seed is considered a fruit, including cucumbers, squash, avocadoes, etc.)

- Consume calcium-rich foods, such as dark green leafy vegetables, sesame seeds, flax seeds, almonds, molasses, brocolli, figs, dulse, kelp, carob, and brewer's yeast to strengthen your bones and teeth.

- Floss at least once a day before brushing the teeth, never reusing the same section of the floss. Brush at least twice a day (but no more than three times) using a soft-bristled toothbrush. Brushing includes your tongue, the inside of your cheeks and the roof of your mouth. Change toothbrushes every thirty days and after healing from an illness. Rinse mouth with water after consuming acidic food or drinks.

- Shifting of the teeth occurs due to lack of mineralization. For example, our wisdom teeth become crowded and eventually must be removed due to skeletal structural changes (one of many physiological changes) that have occured over generations of eating cooked, denatured, and processed foods. Be certain to include foods with a high mineral content as listed on page **17**.

- See a dentist at least once a year. Be sure to consume kelp and wheatgrass for the x-ray radiation exposure. Find a holistic dentist who is informed and willing to address your concerns. If you do not feel comfortable with their response, find another dentist. Visit www.holisticdental.org for more information.

How to Eat 101

Eating right involves many rules that we break every day and we pay a high price for it. Proper digestion allows us to absorb valuable vitamins and mineral from food. We understand that the "fast food" society in which we live does not allow proper eating habits. Despite this, we must take control of our health by making time to do things the right way. The rules are very simple:

- Find a quiet place where you can focus on eating.

- Give thanks to the Creator for the food and pray that it nourishes you physically, mentally, and spiritually.

- Sit down or squat down versus standing up while eating so your digestive organs will be correctly positioned to properly digest the food.

- Chew your food at least 25 times.

- Eat your heaviest meal in the middle of the day.

- Avoid eating late at night. If you must consume something, eat fruit or drink liquids instead.

- Wait at least 2 hours before going to bed after eating a meal.

- Eat only when you are hungry and stop before you are full.

- Avoid eating and drinking at the same time. Drink 30 minutes before eating or 2 hours after a meal.

- Fruits generally take about 30 minutes to digest and all other foods take about 1 to 2 hours depending on the water content. Improperly combined foods can take 6 or more hours to digest.

- Follow the principles of proper food combining (see chart on page 34 and 35): (a) Melons are best eaten alone (b) Do not eat fruits with any other food. Some exceptions are that apples can be included when juicing vegetables, and lemons combine well with vegetables because their chemical components are generally harmonious with both fruits and vegetables (c) Fruits should not be eaten between meals while other foods are digesting in the stomach. (d) Eat sweet fruits and strongly acidic fruits at separate meals.

Food Combination Chart

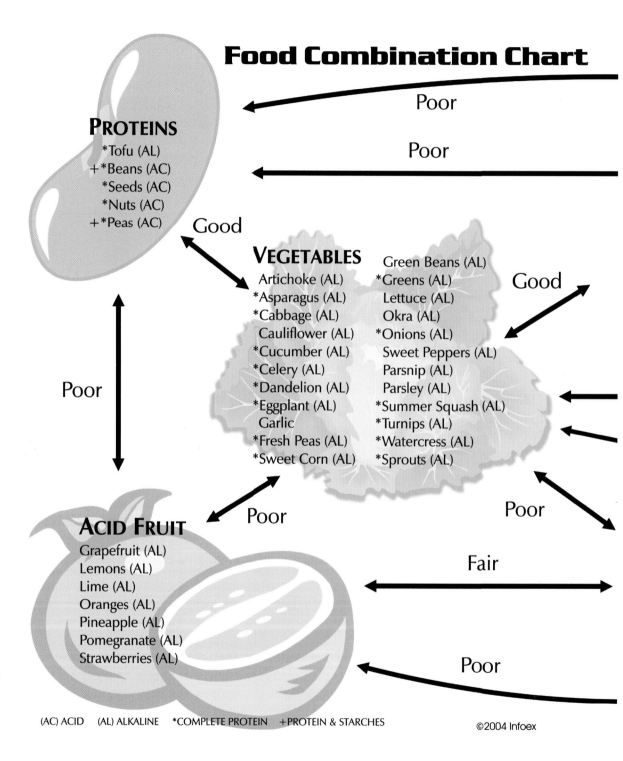

Poor

Poor

PROTEINS
*Tofu (AL)
+*Beans (AC)
*Seeds (AC)
*Nuts (AC)
+*Peas (AC)

Good

VEGETABLES
Artichoke (AL)   Green Beans (AL)
*Asparagus (AL)   *Greens (AL)
*Cabbage (AL)   Lettuce (AL)
Cauliflower (AL)   Okra (AL)
*Cucumber (AL)   *Onions (AL)
*Celery (AL)   Sweet Peppers (AL)
*Dandelion (AL)   Parsnip (AL)
*Eggplant (AL)   Parsley (AL)
Garlic   *Summer Squash (AL)
*Fresh Peas (AL)   *Turnips (AL)
*Sweet Corn (AL)   *Watercress (AL)
                        *Sprouts (AL)

Good

Poor

Poor

Poor

ACID FRUIT
Grapefruit (AL)
Lemons (AL)
Lime (AL)
Oranges (AL)
Pineapple (AL)
Pomegranate (AL)
Strawberries (AL)

Fair

Poor

(AC) ACID   (AL) ALKALINE   *COMPLETE PROTEIN   +PROTEIN & STARCHES

©2004 Infoex

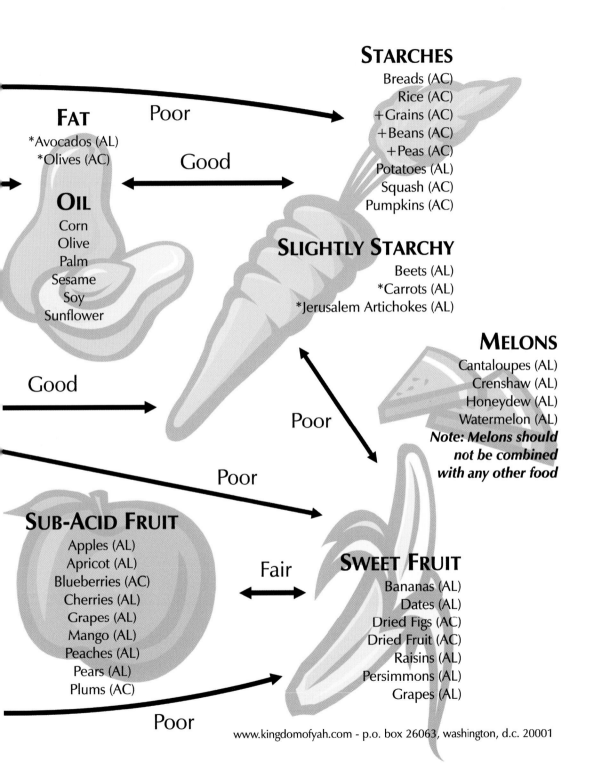

STARCHES
Breads (AC)
Rice (AC)
+Grains (AC)
+Beans (AC)
+Peas (AC)
Potatoes (AL)
Squash (AC)
Pumpkins (AC)

FAT
*Avocados (AL)
*Olives (AC)

Poor

Good

OIL
Corn
Olive
Palm
Sesame
Soy
Sunflower

SLIGHTLY STARCHY
Beets (AL)
*Carrots (AL)
*Jerusalem Artichokes (AL)

MELONS
Cantaloupes (AL)
Crenshaw (AL)
Honeydew (AL)
Watermelon (AL)
*Note: Melons should
not be combined
with any other food*

Good

Poor

Poor

SUB-ACID FRUIT
Apples (AL)
Apricot (AL)
Blueberries (AC)
Cherries (AL)
Grapes (AL)
Mango (AL)
Peaches (AL)
Pears (AL)
Plums (AC)

Fair

SWEET FRUIT
Bananas (AL)
Dates (AL)
Dried Figs (AC)
Dried Fruit (AC)
Raisins (AL)
Persimmons (AL)
Grapes (AL)

Poor

www.kingdomofyah.com - p.o. box 26063, washington, d.c. 20001

A Living Home

The Nutrition Room

The nutrition room is a part of the home set aside for the planning and preparation of the nutritional foods that will sustain and maintain the good health of the family. The preparer of the meal must have a willing spirit, cleanliness, and consistency. When first entering the nutrition room, one should sanctify the area. The hands should be washed and the head should be covered. Make hot dish water and make sure the work space is clean and orderly. Wash all fruits and vegetables before use. As a rule, throw away meals that are 3 days or older unless otherwise indicated to avoid unhealthy incidents. Always read labels on prepackaged foods to avoid additives, preservatives, and meat and dairy products.

Some helpful elements in a raw household are:

The Creator, Love & Creativity

Juicer   Cheesecloth to cover jars

Blender   Dehydrator *(optional)*

Food Processor   Baskets of fruit

Seed Grinder   Herb and spice plants
(aloe vera, basil, lavender)

Sharp Knives

Your own garden *(optional)*

Wooden Cutting Board

Raw food recipe books

Large glass jars for sprouting

Culinary Suggestions

Here are just a few tips to spark your own creativity and make your raw meal extraordinary:

- Balance the taste of the meal between sweet (sweet fruits, vegetables, or natural sweeteners); sour (lemon, apple cider vinegar, etc.), bitter (garlic, ginger, horseradish, etc.), salty (natural salt substitutes and naturally salty foods); and pungent (peppers, cilantro, fenugreek).
- The meal should be served as fresh as possible.
- When presenting the meal, symmetry and balance are key.
- Utilize the food items in the recipes to garnish the meal. Some ideas are sprouts, sliced avocados, fanned strawberries, edible flowers, lemon slices, orange peel curly-ques, parsley sprigs, tomato slices, sprinkles of dried parsley or paprika, drizzling or zig-zagging sauces across the plate, and serving the food on a bed of shredded lettuce or lettuce leaves. Don't go over board. Less is more. Keep it simple.
- Use cookie cutters, jar lids, sculpted bowls, hand molding, and more to add creative shapes to various food dishes.
- To add natural colors to foods, try the following: orange- carrot juice, red- beet juice/powder or paprika, green- spirulina, yellow- turmeric powder, brown- tamari or molasses, purple- purple cabbage, blue- blueberries.
- Be conscious to cut fruits and vegetables into bite-size pieces unless the recipe calls for otherwise.
- If you must have warm food: cover with cheese cloth and set in the sunshine, place food under a warm lamp, warm in a oven set at 200-degrees or less, place in dehydrator set below 110-degrees, blend for an extended period of time, add cayenne pepper or other pungent spices.

Knives

Your knives are one of the most important and potentially dangerous tools in the nutrition room so treat them accordingly. Sharpen knives regularly to preserve their longevity. Dull knives can slip on food and cut the skin. Keep them away from children, the edge of counters, and out of sinks filled with dishwater. Also, dishwater loosens knife handles so always hand wash knives. Store knives in a knife block rather than a cluttered drawer which can dull the blade and cause accidents. Never grab a falling knife, instead, get out of the way. Hold a knife properly for more control and less fatigue: your thumb and index finger should be on opposite sides of the blade while your last three fingers rest on the handle. Always cut on a cutting board. When cutting, keep your eyes on the blade. Avoid walking with knives, but if you must, carry it in your hand at your side with your arm rigid. Keep the point straight down with the blade facing your thigh.

Measurement Chart

Kitchen Math With Metric Table

MEASURE	EQUIVALENT	METRIC (ML)
1 Tbsp.	3 tsp.	14.8 milliliters
2 Tbsp.	1 oz. 2	9.6 milliliters
1 jigger	1 1/2 oz. 4	4.4 milliliters
1/4 cup	4 Tbsp.	59.2 milliliters
11/3 cup	5 Tbsp. plus 1 tsp.	78.9 milliliters
1/2 cup	8 Tbsp.	118.4 milliliters
1 cup	16 Tbsp.	236.8 milliliters
1 pint	2 cups	473.6 milliliters
1 quart	4 cups	947.2 milliliters
1 liter	4 cups plus 3 1/2 Tbsp.	1,000.0 milliliters
1 ounce (dry)	2 Tbsp.	28.35 grams
1 pound	16 oz.	453.59 grams
2.21 pounds	35.3 oz.	1.00 kilogram

The Approximate Conversion Factors For Units Of Volume

To Convert From	To	Multiply By
teaspoons (tsp.)	milliliters (ml)	5
tablespoons (1tbsp.)	milliliters (ml)	15
fluid ounces (fl. oz.)	milliliters (ml)	30
cups (c)	liters (1)	0.24
pints (pt.)	liters (1)	0.47
quarts (qt.)	liters (1)	0.95
gallons (gal)	liters (1)	3.8
milliliters (ml)	fluid ounces (fl. oz.)	0.03
liters (1)	pints (pt.)	2.1
liters (1)	quarts (qts.)	1.06
liters (1)	gallons (gal.)	0.26

Simplified Measures

dash = less than 1/8 teaspoon

3 tsp.= 1 Tbsp.

16 Tbsp. = 1 cup

1 cup = 1/2 pt.

2 cups = 1 pt.

2 pt. (4 c.) = 1 qt.

4qt. (liquid) = 1 gal

8 qt. (solid) = 1 peck

4 pecks = 1 bushel

16 oz. = 1 lb.

If you want to measure part-cups by the tablespoon, remember:

4 Tbsp. = 1/4 cup

5 1/3 Tbsp. = 1/3 cup

8 Tbsp. = 1/2 cup

10 2/3 Tbsp. = 2/3 cup

12 Tbsp. = 3/4 cup

14 Tbsp. = 7/8 cup

Substitutions

So Many Healthier Choices - Salt, Sugar, and Sandwich Bread Alternatives

Instead of Salt, use…

Salt-free Vegetable Seasoning - Adds flavor without raising your blood pressure, page **131**.

Granulated Kelp – A sea vegetable that is high in iodine, calcium, and many vitamins.

Dulse Powder - A reddish sea vegetable containing numerous vitamins and minerals.

Sumac – Reddish spice seasoning made from crushed and dried berries of a bush that grows wild in the Mediterranean. Available at Mediterranean stores.

Zahtar – Spice made from sesame seeds, sumac, and thyme. Available at Mediterranean stores or see recipe page 132.

Nama Shoyu – A raw soy sauce. Available at health food stores.

Liquid Aminos – a liquid protein that is not heated or fermented; derived from soybeans.

Tamari – A dark condiment thicker than soy sauce and derived from soybeans.

Fresh Celery – Good for reducing blood pressure. Finely chop into foods.

Natural Salt Substitute – See recipe page 130.

Instead of Sugar, use…

Dates - Great sweetener for raw desserts.

Dried Figs – A fleshy sweet pear-shaped fruit when that is usually brown and flat when dried.

Raisins - Most commercial brands are from dried seedless grapes. Can be difficult to find seeded variety.

Maple Syrup – Sap from sugar maple trees. Use grade A or B.

Agave Nectar – A cactus sweetener that is 80% fruit sugar that looks like a lighter version honey. Approved for use by diabetics. Available on the internet or in health food stores.

Green Stevia – A natural herbal sweetener. Can be tricky to use, see chart on page **120**.

Blackstrap Molasses – Adds a little sweetness and lots of minerals to food.

Instead of Sandwich Bread, use…

Pita Bread - Flat bread used in Mediterranean dishes

Tortilla Wraps - Purchase the brand with the shortest list of ingredients.

Homemade Matzo - Does not contain leavening (baking powder, baking soda, etc.) Mix 1 cup of unbleached flour with water. Until mixture is soft, dry and holds together. Season to taste. Roll with a rolling pin and cook in a oiled skilled for a few minutes on each side.

Nori Sheets - Sea vegetables used for sushi. Cooked sheets are green; raw sheets are purple.

Rice Wraps - Flat, paper-thin dried sheets of rice flour and water. Can be purchased at Asian markets. Great for live spring rolls.

Portabello Mushrooms - Remove stems and it becomes a beautiful choice for raw burgers.

Lettuce Leaves - A light choice for making sandwiches, wraps and rolling live burritos.

Cabbage Leaves - Use softer leaves to wrap sandwiches. Can be marinated and dried for flavor.

Eggplant Slices - Peel and slice length-wise for a "submarine" sandwich and cross-wise for a "burger."

Sprouted Wheat Bread - Process sprouted wheatberries (See **How to Sprout,** page 25.) through a Champion juicer with a blank plate or a homogenizer or in a food processor using the s-blade. Season to taste: try adding dates and/or soaked sun-dried tomatoes. Form into desired shape. Dry in a dehydrator at 105 degrees for 4 hours on each side.

Herbs and Spices

Fresh herbs and spices not only flavor the food, but they have medicinal properties as well. They should be consumed in small quantities. See <u>Herbal Medicine</u> by Dian Buchman, PhD for more information. Use this guide to aid you in your tasty healthy live food creations.

Allspice - The berry of a West Indian tree, allspice is mildly pungent, and tastes like a combination of cinnamon, nutmeg, and cloves. Use it to flavor sweet potato or pumpkin pies, pickled foods, carrots, eggplant, cookies, cakes, and relishes. Made into a paste, it relieves toothaches and serves as a mouthwast to freshen the breath.

Anise - An aromatic seed of the carrot family with a licorice flavor, ground anise seed is good sprinkled on cookies. Aids in upper respiratory problems, nausea, and sluggish digestion. Helpful during a bronchial asthma attack. Destroys lice and itching insects.

Basil - A member of the mint family, basil leaf is used in raw soups, tomato dishes, sauces and salads. Relieves delayed menstruation and allieviates the pain of instect stings.

Bay Leaf - From the bay tree, bay leaf is fragrant and pungent. Adds flavor to soups. Allieviates stomach problems, flatulence, aches and pains.

Caraway Seed - A member of the carrot family, the pungent fruit of the caraway is used to flavor rye bread, crackers, and sauerkraut. Digestive aid in adults and infants.

Cardamon Seed - This seed of an Indian plant known as peppergrass comes in capsular pods. Cardamon lends a sweet flavor to breads, cookies, pickles, and curried dishes. Good for diabetes and digestive problems.

Cayenne - The crushed or powdered fruit pods and seeds of hot peppers. Use it in spicy foods, curries, chili, and anything that needs a kick. Contains vitamin C and prevents the flu. Aids in digestion, sore throat, circulation, and cold feet.

Celery Seed - A European herb in the carrot family, celery seed adds flavor to salads, soups, tomatoes, salad dressings.

Chervil - An herb in the carrot family, chervil leaf adds pungent flavor to salads, soups, sauces, and greens. Blend it with cheese; use it like parsley. Helps high blood pressure and digestion. A diuretic and eyewash.

Chive - A perennial plant related to onion, chive is used in salads, and anywhere a mild onion flavor is needed. Known for helping alleviate high blood pressure.

Cilantro - The fresh leaves of coriander, an aromatic herb in the carrot family, cilantro is used as a seasoning in soups, Mexican and Mediterranean foods. Soothes stomach, allieviates gas and pain from rheumatism.

Cinnamon - The bark of a tree in the laurel family, cinnamon is a sweet, aromatic seasoning for apple pie, apple sauce, fruit salads, squash, and some sauces and curries. Helps diarrhea and nausea. Protects against the flu and is a mild astringent.

Clove - The dried flower of a tree in the myrtle family, clove is sweet and very pungent. Helps nausea and depression. Its oil is a temporary skin anesthetic, sleep aid. Powdered clove allieviates pain from a finger cut. Also an insect repellant.

Coriander - The ripened dried fruit of an aromatic herb in the carrot family, coriander seed tastes like a combination of lemon peel and sage. Use it in raw spice cakes, Indian food, live soups, sauces, and sprouted lentil dishes. Warms the stomach, relieves flatulence and aids with chills and fever.

Cumin - The ripened dried fruit of an herb in the carrot family, cumin seed gives an aromatic taste to curries, vegetables and nut loaves. It has a strong flavor, use it sparingly. A liver tonic and allieviates gas.

Dill Weed - An herb in the carrot family, dill seed used for pickling soups and sauces. Has tranquilizing abilities and allieviates constipation. Relieves colic and gas in infants. Increases milk in nursing mothers.

Fennel - A perennial herb in the carrot family, fennel leaf and seed are used in Spanish and Italian dishes and live soups. The seed has a sweet, slightly licorice taste. A diuretic that allieviates gas and aids in detoxification.

Garlic - An aromatic bulbous herb related to onion, garlic contains cloves used fresh, dried, whole, or powdered. Add it to just about any nut or vegetable dish, live soups, and salads. See **Detoxification**, page **27**.

Ginger - The thick pungent root of a widely cultivated tropical plant, ginger is used in Chinese, Japanese, and Indian cuisine, in chutneys, pickles, apple sauce, raw cookies, pies, and cakes. Digestive aid, prevents colds, aids in circulation, and stimulates a delayed menstrual cycle.

Mace - The dried, external fibrous covering of nutmeg seed, mace is sweet and aromatic. Use in raw pies and cakes.

Marjoram - A member of the mint family, marjoram leaf is used in stuffings, soups, and salad dressings. A mild tonic, lessens fever, headaches, swelling, rheumatism, and sore throat. Helps most digestive problems.

Mint - A highly aromatic herb, mint leaf contains menthol, which is cool and refreshing. Use fresh or dried in drinks, salads, live soups, fruit salad, and anywhere a cool aromatic flavor is desired. Peppermint helps relieve headaches, muscle spasms, cramps, digestive problems, and sinus problems.

Nutmeg - The fruit of a tree native to the Indonesian Spice Islands, nutmeg is used in custards, pudding, live pumpkin and fruit pies, and nogs. It is aromatic and slightly bitter. Assists a sluggish digestion, flatulence (gas) and diarrhea.

Oregano - A bushy perennial of the mint family, oregano leaf is used in Italian food, live soups, chili, tomato sauce, and in marinades. Good for coughs, headaches, urinary problems, indigestion, and gas.

Paprika - The ground, dried fruit of various sweet peppers, paprika is used as a garnish to add a red color. Excellent source of beta carotene which the body converts to vitamin A.

Parsley - An all-purpose herb of the carrot family, parsley is used in salads, vegetables, soups, non-dairy cheeses, and as a garnish. A diuretic. See **Seven Daily Whole Food Supplements**, page **17**.

Poppy Seed - The seed of the poppy flower has a nutlike flavor. Use poppy seed for live cakes and sprouted breads. Different variaties may alliviate congestion, can also serve as a mild sedative and pain reliever.

Rosemary - A fragrant shrub of the mint family, rosemary leaf adds a delicate, slightly bitter flavor to nut loaves, soups and salads. Helps allieviate colds, headaches, and bad breath. Good for the, stomach, skin, and memory.

Saffron - The rare and expensive dried stigmas of the purple crocus flower, saffron imparts flavor and a bright yellow color to rice, Spanish dishes, and curry sauces. Useful for coughs, gas, and gastrointestinal problems.

Sage - A grayish shrub in the mint family, sage leaf adds a spicy aroma and taste to soups and vegetables. Aids in depression, sleep, bad breath, flu, skin problems, stomach problems, vericose veins and leg ulcers.

Savory - Two members of the mint family, summer savory and winter savory, are used in green beans, salads, stuffings, cabbage dishes, and soups. A mild astringent that is helpful for diarrhea, gas, and sore throats.

Tarragon - The leaf of a small perennial wormword plant, tarragon is used to flavor vinegars, tartar sauce, salad greens, and vegetables. Aids in prevention of cancer and viruses. Aids in expelling intestinal worms in children.

Thyme - A member of the mint family, thyme leaf imparts a fresh aroma to sauces, tomato dishes, soups, and stuffings. Allieviates uterine problems, gastric problems, headaches, lung congestions, sore throat, and fever. Also an insect repellant and anticeptic.

Turmeric - The brilliant yellow root of an East Indian perennial herb, turmeric adds slight flavor and a yellow color to curries, live cakes, sprouted breads, raw cookies, and grain dishes. Good for wounds and bacterial infections, has anti-cancer properties and aids in digestion.

Vanilla - The fruit of a tropical climbing orchid, vanilla "bean", its extract, or seeds are used in live desserts and syrups.

A Blessing Before Meals

A prayer of blessing before meals gives thanks to the Creator (Yah) for blessing us with dietary consciousness based on the eternal idea of Genesis 1:29. The prayer is that the heavenly manna we are provided with will regenerate our souls and minds, sustain true life and strengthen us so we can fulfill the holy will of Yah forever and ever.

English
Blessed by Yah (God of Israel). King of the Universe, Who brings forth bread from the earth. Thank you Father for this nourishment. Sel-ah.

Hebrew (Phonetics)
Ba-rook Ah-tah Yah-h-wah Me-lek- ha-O-lam. Ha-mot-see Le-khem Meen Ha-ah-retz. To-dah Ahb-ba Bish-vil Ha-ma-zone Ha-zeh. Se-lah.

Beverages

Fresh Grape Juice

Ripe Grapes with seeds.

Wash grapes. You can juice one of two ways:

(1) In a bowl, use your bare hands to squeeze out some of the juice from the grapes. Next, place the pulp into a cheesecloth and squeeze out the juice into a bowl.

(2) Or, put grapes into a blender and blend on pulse setting. Press juice through a strainer into a bowl.

Pour juice into a pitcher, chill and serve.

A wonderful internal cleanser, grapes contain iron, vitamin C and are good for the lungs and liver. Remember: all fruits and vegetables taste best when fresh, organic, ripe and in season. Always wash before consuming.

Fresh Watermelon Juice

1 Watermelon with seeds, cut out of the rind

Cut watermelon into chunks. Using your hands, crush the chunks to squeeze out juice through a strainer into a bowl. Pour juice into a pitcher, lightly chill and serve.

Watermelons have one of the highest water content of any food and high in vitamin C.

47

Kale-Apple-Celery Juice

1 Bunch Kale
1 Cucumber
1 Apple
2 Stalks of Celery

Juice and drink immediately. One of my favorite juices.

Serves 2

Carrot-Spinach-Celery Juice

2 Carrots
2 Stalks of Celery
1 bunch of Spinach
1 bunch of Parsley

Same as directions above. Good for headaches, and some skin and blood disorders.

Serves 1

Raspberry-Blackberry Juice

1 Cup fresh ripe Raspberries
1 Cup fresh ripe Blackberries
Sweetener (optional)

Blend and strain. This juice is helpful for diarrhea, mouth sores, digestion, menstrual cramps, and nausea.

Serves 1

JUICING

Juices are excellent energy drinks that give your body concentrated vitamins and minerals without taxing your digestive system.

If you are new to juicing, begin by diluting juices with one part water to two parts juice. Avoid mixing fruit and vegetable juices together. Apples are an exception.

How to drink juices: *Slowly sip so it does not overload your kidneys. Allow it to mix with the juices in your mouth to aid in digestion, then swallow.*

Never drink straight beet juice because the powerful iron content will go straight to your head. Juices containing green leafy vegetables should be consumed in small quantities and mixed with other vegetables until your body becomes use to their power.

Precautions: *If you have a sugar-related illness, kidney problems, or are pregnant or nursing, check with your health care professional before juicing.*

Rejuvalac

1 cup Wheatberries, sprouted 2 days, see **"How to Sprout"** page **25**
Purified Water

In a sprouting jar, add 3 cups of purified water to the sprouted wheatberries. Cover with cheesecloth and secure with a rubberband. Allow to sit at room temperature for 2 days. Keeping the cheesecloth covering intact, gently pour water into another glass container. Refill the jar with more purified water over the wheatberries and allow to sit for another day. Pour this water into another glass container and refill the wheat berry jar one last time with water and sit for one day. Discard wheatberries after pouring off this third batch of rejuvalac.
Store rejuvalac in a refrigerator and discard after two or three days or it can become toxic to the body. Also discard if liquid has a foul smell. Rejuvalac should be grown under very sanitary conditions. It may be consumed in place of water and may be consumed with meals because it aids in digestion. Adding it to cabbage juice is wonderful for ulcers and stomach disorders.

*Excellent health drink that aids digestion and adds good healthy
bacteria to the body. High in vitamin B, C, and E.*

Wheatgrass (Grow your own)

1 cup Wheatberries, sprouted 1 day
2- 9" x 12" trays
Good quality organic soil
1 tablespoon powdered Kelp
Wheatgrass Juicer

In a bucket, mix soil with kelp to add trace minerals. Wheatgrass absorbs nutrients that are put into the soil. Spread a 1-inch layer of soil on a tray, leaving a small trench around the edges for water drainage. Evenly spread wheatberries over soil making sure they are not on top of one another. Dampen (do not soak) soil, cover with second tray, and store at room temperature. Allow growth for 3 days before placing in direct sunlight. Check periodically for moisture in the soil. If mold forms, throw it out and try again using less water and a cooler temperature. Your wheatgrass is ready when it reaches a height of 7-inches. Juice in a manual or electric wheatgrass juicer. Wheatgrass should be consumed immediately after juicing to avoid spoilage. If you are new to wheatgrass, begin by drinking just 1-ounce a day. You can cut grasses and store in a refrigerator for up to seven days. Do not rinse grasses before storing.

According to The Wheatgrass Book by Ann Wigmore, wheatgrass has numerous uses:

- Prevents graying hair
- Removes heavy metals
- Purifies tap water
- Detoxifies the body
- Great for anemia
- Clears skin problems
- Lowers high blood pressure
- Aids in digestion
- Alleviates constipation
- Stabilizes blood sugar levels
- Heals scar tissue
- Can restore fertility
- Prevents tooth decay
- Clears a sore throat
- Acts as a deodorant
- Has 20 more different uses

Brazilian Nut Milk

1 cup Brazil Nuts, soaked overnight
3 cups purified Water
2 Bananas
3 tablespoons Maple Syrup
3 tablespoons Vanilla Flavor

Brazil nuts have a high mineral content (especially calcium) because they have never been domesticated.

Blend all ingredients at the highest speed until smooth. Strain into a pitcher through cheesecloth.

House of Mahneel

Almond Nut Milk

1 cup Almonds with or without skins, soaked overnight
3 cups filtered Water
2 Bananas (optional)
3 tablespoons Maple Syrup
1 tablespoon Vanilla flavor

Place all ingredients in a blender and blend at the highest speed until smooth. Strain through cheesecloth.

House of Mahneel

Removing Almond Skins
Soak almonds in hot water, then pinch the nut and they will slide out of their skins.

Sesame Seed Milk

1 cup soaked or sprouted Sesame Seeds, unhulled
2 cups filtered Water
1 ripe Banana

Blend sesame seeds in a seed grinder or high speed blender. Blend seeds with water and banana.

A good calcium drink that curbs your sugar craving.

Sprouted Soy Milk

1 cup Soybeans, soaked and sprouted 1 day
2 cups Water
2 tablespoons Maple Syrup

Blend soybeans and water until creamy. Strain liquid through a cheesecloth. Add sweetener. Save pulp for tofu recipes.

Soaking and sprouting increase the digestibility of soybeans.

Delicious Citrus Shake

1 pound of Tangerines
10 large Strawberries
3 or 4 Kiwis, peeled and chopped

Juice the tangerines and put in a blender with strawberries and kiwis. Blend until smooth.

Bilgah Baht Israel

Serves 2

Citrus fruits have cancer-fighting properties. Perfect fruit for the winter months to boost immune system.

Mango Shake

2 Mangos
1 cup Fruit Juice
½ cup Ice

Blend.

Mangos are good for the skin, hair, bones, eyes, and reproductive system. Remember: a mango with no scent has no flavor.

Serves 1

Young Coconut Water

1 Young Coconut (large green variety not the brown hairy type)
Big sharp knife

In the absence of a machete (and experience in using one), carefully chop the coconut skin with a big sharp knife, cutting away from you until reaching the softer inner shell. Pierce inner shell and drink the liquid. Now wasn't all that hard work worth it? The liquid can also be used for shakes and marinades.

Note: To open the brown hairy variety (if young coconuts are not available), pierce the eyes of the coconut with a hammer and nail and drain the water. Place coconut in a plastic bag and hit with a hammer. Cut away meat with a pairing knife.

Nutritional Value of Coconuts

- Good nutrition source for children
- Good body fat builder
- Excellent source of lipids
- Blood builder
- Energy Increaser
- Increases semen
- Good for the heart
- One of the purest most alkaline sources of water

Power Shake

2 cups **Sesame Seed Milk**, recipe page **52**
1 ripe Banana, peeled
1 Tablespoon Brewer's Yeast
2 Tablespoon Raw Carob Powder
1 teaspoon Spirulina
½ cup Ice
Maple Syrup to taste

Blend.

Serves 2

Spirulina
This micro algae is one of the highest known source of vitamin B-12; an easy to digest vegetable protein; high in iron, magnesium trace minerals; an excellent source of beta carotene.

Breakfast

Apple Sauce

3 Apples, peeled, cored & chopped
Purified Water or Apple Juice

Place apples in blender on pulse setting and add liquid until the desired consistency is achieved.

Apples clean the liver, soften gall stones, and aid colon function. Fresh is always better. Most bottled apple sauces have preservatives or stabilizers to maintain the light color of the apples.

Apple-Mango Soup

2 Mangos
4 Apples, cored & peeled
1/8 banana, peeled and chopped

Blend mangoes and apples. Serve in a bowl. Decorate with banana chunks.

Serves 2

Raw Cereal with Apple Juice

4 cups Oats
½ cup Pumpkin Seeds
1 cup Black Raisins
1 cup Yellow Raisins
½ cup Sunflower Seeds
2 cups Date Pieces
½ cup Flax Seeds
1 cup Cashews
½ cup Almond Slices
Apple Juice

Tastes best with apple juice, but can be eaten with seed milks, nut milks, soy milk or soaked in water with a natural sweetener added. Tip: Makes a nice trail mix minus the oatmeal, flax seeds and apple juice.

Thoroughly mix all ingredients except for the apple juice. Remove the portion that will be eaten and soak in apple juice for at least 30 minutes.

Serves 10

Onam Ben Israel

Hebrew Fruit Salad with Sauce

2 Apples, diced
2 Bananas, peeled and sliced
¼ cup Raisins, soaked 30 minutes and drained
Cashew pieces, soaked overnight and drained

Sauce:
1 cup mixture Apples, Bananas, Raisins
¼ cup Nut or Seed Milk or Purified Water
2 Tablespoons Agave Nectar

In a bowl, mix apples, bananas, and raisins. Scoop out 1 cup of the fruit mixture and blend with liquid and agave nectar. Pour on sauce. Mmmm. Good.

Serves 1 hungry soul

Flax Cereal

2 tablespoons Flax Seeds, sprouted 2 days
2 Apples, peeled and chopped
2 Dates, pitted and chopped

Mix and serve.

Serves 1

This is a good first cereal for babies.

Melon Melody

1 Watermelon slice
½ Honey Dew Melon, halved, remove seeds
½ Cantaloupe, halved, remove seeds

Scoop out flesh of each melon with an ice cream scooper to make round balls. Set honey dew and cantaloupe shells aside. Fill shells with scoops of all of the melons.

Serves 2

Melons have one of the highest water contents of any food, so they are highly-digestible and a perfect choice for hot weather. They should not be combined with other foods because they have a very short digestion time.

Mango-Banana Salad (Blend or eat)

2 ripe juicy Mangos, diced
2 ripe Bananas, cut in round slices

Mix and serve. This fruit can also be blended with nut or seed milk for a nice shake.

Serves 2

Cleansing Citrus Salad

4 Oranges, peeled
2 Grapefruits, peeled
2 tablespoons Agave Nectar, see page 40.

Cut oranges and grapefruit in half, remove seeds and pull apart each section. If grapefruit skin is tough, separate from pulp and discard. Add agave nectar and mix well.

Serves 2

Citrus fruits boost the immune system, aid in digestion, clean the blood and liver, and fight against cancer (sustain life).

Citrus Twist Salad

2 Mangos, cubed
2 Tangerines, halved, peeled & seeded
1 Pineapple, halved including the crown
Strawberries (if not sweet, marinate in a little agave nectar), sliced

Pull tangerine slices apart. Remove pineapple pulp while preserving the shell and dice. Mix mangos, pineapple, and tangerines. Serve in a pineapple half. Decorate with sliced strawberries.

Serves 2

Brilliant Buckwheat

1 cup Buckwheat, soaked overnight or
sprouted 1 day
3 tablespoons Olive Oil
¼ cup Nutritional Yeast
1 teaspoon Sea Salt

Buckwheat is a non-mucous forming herb (often mistaken for a grain) that increases blood circulation. It is great for those with diabetes because it stabilizes blood-sugar levels.

Mix and enjoy.

Serves 2

Soaked Oats

1 cup Oatmeal
¼ cup Raisins
½ teaspoon Cinnamon
1 Apple, diced
1 Banana, sliced
1 cup Water
Maple Syrup to taste

Presoak oatmeal in water for about 30 minutes. Mix with sweetener and cinnamon. Stir in apple, banana, and raisins.

Serves 1

Oatmeal

Whole:	must be sprouted before consuming.
Steel Cut:	an oat groat cut in half. Soak before consuming.
Rolled:	flattened whole oats. Soak before consuming.

Lunch

Vibrant Live Soup

4 Kale leaves, stems removed
1 Avocado, peeled, pitted, and diced
1 cup Sprouts
2 stalks Celery
½ small Red Onion
1 Garlic Clove
1 Cucumber, peeled
½ cup Carrot Juice
1 tablespoon Flax Seed Oil
1 tablespoon Nama Shoyu Sauce

Chop all vegetables. Place all ingredients into a blender and blend for about 31 seconds. Decorate with sliced scallions and a thinly sliced tomato.

Serves 2

Living Tomato Soup

1 pound fresh Tomatoes
7 fresh Basil leaves
1 tablespoon of Liquid Aminos
2 Scallions (Spring Onions)
Add other fresh vegetables of your choice

Chop and blend all ingredients together. For a chunky soup, set aside a portion of the chopped tomatoes and add to soup after blending.

Serves 4

Bilgah Baht Israel

Sprouted Soup

2 cups Sprouts of your choice
2 cups purified water
7 Spinach leaves
1 Avocado, peeled and diced
1 tablespoon Kelp Powder
Liquid Aminos

Blend well.

Serves 4

Brothy Vegetable Soup

2 Cups Purified Water
6 paper-thin round slices of Carrot, use mandolin slicer
6 paper-thin round slices of Zucchini, use mandolin slicer
4 Shitake Mushrooms, thinly sliced
¼ cup Jicama, peeled, julienned
1 Lemon, juiced
3 tablespoons Liquid Aminos
2 leaves of fresh Basil, sliced
1 tablespoon Arame Seaweed
¼ cup Scallion (Green Onion)
1 tablespoon Maple Syrup
1 teaspoon Dulse

Combine ingredients.

Serves 2

Edenic Salad

1 head of Lettuce, chopped fine
1 Tomato, diced
1 Carrot, shredded
1 Cucmber, peeled & sliced
¼ cup Purple Cabbage, shredded
2 marinated Artichokes, pulled apart
1 Avocado, peeled, pitted and diced
1 handful Brown Olives, pitted and sliced

Thoroughly mix lettuce, cabbage, carrots and cucmber. Top with tomatoes, artichoke hearts, avocados and olives. Serve with your favorite dressing.

Serves 8 to 10

A Perfect Salad: The key is a mixture of texture and flavors. After washing lettuce leaves, drain, pat or spin dry so salad remains crisp. When storing salad in refrigerator, place a damp paper towel at the bottom of the container to maintain humidity. Remember: Iceburg lettuce has no nutritional value.

Raw Tofu (Make your own)

1 cup Soybeans
2 cups Water

Soak soy beans for 12 hours. Drain. Soak for another 12 hours. Blend soybeans with 2 cups of water until creamy. Set aside and allow to ferment for 8 hours at room temperature. Press curds through cheesecloth to squeeze out liquid. Shape into blocks. Store in a plastic bag in a refrigerator. Use within 2 days. Season and add to sandwiches, salads, soups and more.

Vegetable Sandwich

1 medium, thin Eggplant, peeled, sliced length-wise
1 cup **Sun-Dried Tomato Nut Pate**, recipe page **67**.
1 Cucumber, peeled and sliced
Spinach leaves, stems removed
1 Red Onion
Tomatoes slices
Sunflower Sprouts
Parsley, destemmed
Or your favorite vegetables
Your favorite sauce, see "**Spice It Up**" section page **129**.

Assemble and enjoy!

Makes about 4 sandwiches

A great way to eat your vegetables when traveling.

Avocado Sandwich

Sprouted Wheat Bread, recipe page **41**
1 Avocado, peeled, pitted, and sliced
2 Tomato slices
1 Lettuce Leaf
Alfalfa Sprouts
Nut Mayo, recipe page **136**

Avocados
contain protein, potassium, and vitamin E; a good way for raw foodists to gain and maintain weight.

Assemble and enjoy!

Sun-Dried Tomato Nut Pate

2 cups Pecans, soaked 1 hour and drained
1 cup Sun-dried Tomatoes, soaked in warm water
1 small ripe juicy Tomato
1 stalks Celery, chopped
½ Red Bell Pepper, chopped
¼ small Red Onion, chopped
¼ cup Nutritional Yeast
1 tablespoon Sage
1 tablespoon Cumin
1 tablespoon Basil
Liquid Aminos to Taste

Grind nuts in food processor and pour into a bowl. Place all remaining ingredients in food processor or blender and chop at high speed. Gradually add mixture to nuts and mix until reaching desired texture.

Makes Approximately 2 cups

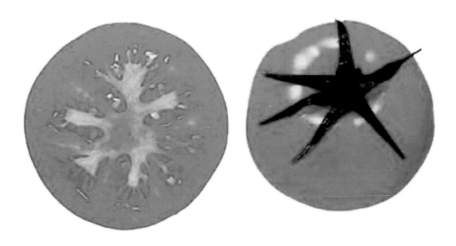

Sliced Cashew Cheese

¼ cup Cashews, soaked
5 tablespoons Agar-agar
1 ½ cups Purified Water
½ Red Bell Pepper
¼ cup Nutritional Yeast
3 tablespoons fresh Lemon Juice
2 tablespoons Tahini
2 Teaspoons Diced Onion
¼ Teaspoon Brown Mustard Seeds, ground
1 Teaspoon Sea Salt

Boil water and remove from flame. Stir in agar-agar and allow it to dissolve and cool before adding remaining ingredients. (NOTE: Do not allow the mixture to sit to cool for too long or it will become solid.) Blend all ingredients in a blender at high speed. Oil a small glass dish with olive oil and pour in mixture. Refrigerate for at least 1 hour so cheese will hold it's shape. Remove from dish. Slice and serve.

Blend.

Serves 10

What is Agar-Agar?
It is prepared from several species of red algae (or seaweed). This additive is used as a texturizing agent, emulsifier, stabilizing agent and thickener in ice cream, sherbets, jellies, soups, sauces, canned soups, and cheese. It is a vegetable gelatin, and is therefore used by vegetarians because true gelatin is made from leftover part of animals.

Flax Crackers

2 cups Flax Seeds, soaked 5 hours in 2 cups water
1 cup Sun-Dried Tomatoes, soaked 1 hour, chopped
1 Garlic Clove, minced
1 teaspoon Sea Salt
1 Lemon, juiced

Mix ingredients. Spread a thin layer on teflex sheet of dehydrator. Dehydrate at 105-degrees for 4 hours. Flip crackers, remove teflex sheet, and dehydrate for 5 hours or until crisp.

Why Dehydrate?

Dehydrators use a fan to blow hot air on food to remove the water content. When the water is removed, the taste is more concentrated. Dehydrating foods adds versatility to recipes as one is transitioning to a live diet. It can also cut costs for certain foods items because fresh foods that you purchase and dehydrate yourself are generally less expensive (and healthier) than pre-dried foods. If you live in a hot climate, your costs decrease even more because instead of purchasing a dehydrator, you can use the sunshine. Try drying your own fruits, vegetable broths, sun-dried tomatoes, herbs and spices. Soak and dehydrate nuts to remove enzyme inhibitors; making them more digestible while preserving the taste.

Pizza Wrap

Tortilla Wrap
¼ Red Bell Pepper, sliced
1/8 small Red Onion, sliced
Mushrooms, sliced
Spinach leaves, stems removed
Your favorite vegetables

Sun-Dried Tomato Sauce, recipe page **134**.

Sunshine Cheese, recipe page **136**.

Place vegetables in wrap, add as much sauce and cheese as desired and wrap it up!

Live Pizza

Sun-Dried Tomato Sauce, recipe page **134**.

Sunshine Cheese, recipe page **136**.

Crust:
2 cups Almonds, finely ground
¼ cup Flax Seeds, ground
10 Sun-Dried Tomatoes, soaked and drained
Purified Water

Place crust ingredients in a food processor on high speed until well mixed. Add a little water so crust will hold together. Lightly oil a pan with olive oil and spread on mixture. Smooth into a ¼-inch crust. Top with sauce, cheese and vegetables.

Spinach Roll

Rice Wraps
1 pound Spinach, stems removed, finely chopped
2 Avocados, peeled and pitted
2 Tablespoon Nama Shoyu or 1 teaspoon Sea Salt
½ Red Onion, chopped
2 Tablespoon Extra Virgin Olive Oil
1 Tablespoon Garlic
1 teaspoon **Vegetable Seasoning**, recipe page **131.**

Spinach is good for the eyes and can alleviate constipation.

Soak 1 rice wrap sheet in a shallow plate with water. Drain. Mix vegetables and seasonings. Place a handful of spinach mixture in center of wrap. Shape into log. Fold one end of wrap over the log. Bring sides together. Roll to the open end. Allow roll to sit on the seam to seal closed. Repeat the process until all of the mixture is wrapped. Serve with Maple Mustard Sauce.

Makes about 15 rolls.

Sunshine Burger

1 cup Sunflower Seeds, ground
1 cup fresh Carrot Pulp
10 pieces of Sun-Dried Tomatoes, soaked & chopped fine
1 Garlic Clove, chopped
1 tablespoon Maple Syrup
1 teaspoon Cumin
1 teaspoon Sage
1 teaspoon Sea Salt

Sunflower seeds are high in protein and unsaturated fat.

Mix and shape into burger. If mixture is too wet, add more ground sunflower seeds. Eat with a salad, make it into a sandwich with your favorite vegetable toppings, or roll it in a nori sheet with avocado slices. Delicious!

Serves 4

Kale & Avocado Salad

1 bunch Kale Greens
1 Avocado, diced

2 tablespoons Liquid Aminos
¼ cup Nutritional Yeast
1 tablespoon fresh Lemon juice

1/4 cup Extra Virgin Olive Oil
4 Garlic Cloves

Wash kale and chop in a food processor using the slicer blade. Blend a paste of olive oil and garlic. In a bowl, mix kale, liquid aminos, nutritional yeast, lemon juice and as much of the garlic paste as desired. Add diced avocado. Decorate with tomato slices. To your health!

Serves 4

Spinach Salad

1 pound Spinach, stems removed
2 Garlic Cloves, sliced thin
¼ cup Fresh Lemon Juice
¼ cup Extra Virgin Olive Oil
1 Tomato, sliced and quartered
¼ cup Brown Olives, pitted and sliced

Wash spinach. Mix with remaining ingredients thoroughly and share with someone you love.

Serves 4

Olive Oil should be cold-pressed extra virgin because it maintains its chlorophyll. Heating olive oil makes it difficult to digest (toxic).

Green Quiche

2 pounds Swiss Chard
4 medium Tomatoes, thinly sliced
1 tablespoon Turmeric
1 teaspoon Sumac

Crust:
½ cup Flax Seeds, ground
½ cup Sesame Seeds, ground
1 tablespoon granulated Garlic
½ teaspoon Cayenne Pepper
1 teaspoon Dulse
¼ teaspoon Kelp Powder

Cheese:
1 cup Tahini
1 tablespoon Turmeric
½ Lemon, juiced
2 Cloves of Garlic, pressed.

Remove stems from Swiss Chard and shred leaves. Mix with Turmeric and Sea Salt. In a separate bowl, mix together crust ingredients and press into an 8-inch pie dish. Blend cheese ingredients in a blender. Inside crust, layer sliced tomatoes, cheese, swiss chard, and repeat the process again, ending with a top layer of cheese. Chill, slice and eat.

Serves 8

House of Mahneel

For definitions of dulse, kelp, and sumac, see page **40**.

Live Spinach Quiche

1 pound Spinach
½ medium Red Onion, chopped
½ pint Button Mushrooms, sliced
½ cup **Sunshine Cheese** recipe, page **139**.
2 Garlic Cloves, minced
½ teaspoon nutmeg
1/8 teaspoon Cayenne Pepper
Liquid Aminos to taste

Crust:
½ cup shredded Coconut
½ cup Pecans, ground
1/8 teaspoon Nutmeg
Mix together thoroughly and press into an 8-inch pie dish.

Clean spinach thoroughly, remove stems, chop fine and marinate with onion and mushrooms in liquid aminos and spices for 15 minutes. Mix with cheese. Press crust into a pie dish and fill with spinach mixture.

Serves 8

Zvenah Eshet Sar Elyahshuv

Barbecued Mushrooms

2 cups Cremini Mushrooms (Baby Portabellos), sliced
Liquid Aminos to taste

Barbecue sauce:
1 cup **Sun-Dried Tomato Sauce**, recipe page **134**.
1 tablespoon Molasses
1 tablespoon Maple Syrup

Lightly spray mushrooms with liquid aminos. Mix with barbecue sauce and serve.

Spaghetti

1- 8 ounce pack of dried Bean Thread Noodles
¼ cup Nama Shoyu
¼ cup Extra Virgin Olive Oil
2 cups **Sun-Dried Tomato Sauce**, recipe page **134**.
7 Mushrooms, sliced
1 Red Bell Pepper, thinly sliced
1 Red Onion, thinly sliced
½ small Yellow Squash, paper-thin slices
½ small Zucchini, paper-thin slices

Boil water and remove from flame. Immediately add bean thread noodles and soak for 1 hour. Marinate vegetables in nama shoyu. Drain noodles and use a sharp knife to cut strands. Mix with liquid aminos. When serving, top noodles with marinated vegetables and tomato sauce.

Serves 2

Vegetable Lasagna

2 medium Zucchini
2 ears fresh Yellow Sweet Corn, kernels cut from cob
1 cup Spinach Leaves, stems removed
1 Portabello Mushroom, stem removed
2 tablespoons Olive Oil
Liquid Aminos

2 cups **Sunshine Cheese**, recipe page **136**.
2 cups **Sun-Dried Tomato Sauce**, recipe page **134**.

Brown Olives, pitted sliced
Extra Virgin Olive Oil

Use a mandolin slicer to slice zucchini into paper-thin slices. Reserve for "noodles." Slice the mushrooms and marinate with a little liquid aminos. In a separate bowl, mix spinach with a little olive oil and liquid aminos. Lightly oil a small 9x7x2 inch casserole dish with olive oil. Layer the lasagna in the following manner: zucchini (2 layers: one layer horizontal, one vertical), spinach, sauce, corn, zucchini (2 layers), spinach, cheese, mushrooms, zucchini (2 layers), spinach, sauce, corn, zucchini (2 layers), and cheese. Decorate with sliced olives. Serve immediately. Note: the longer the lasagna sits, the more juice runs out. One technique I use is to serve it on a bed of lettuce.

Serves 5

Southern Soul

Pecan Loaf with Tomato Sauce

4 cups Pecans
1 Red Bell Pepper, finely chopped
1/2 large Red Onion, finely chopped
3 Stalks of Celery, finely chopped
3 tablespoons Cumin
1 tablespoon Garlic Granules
1 tablespoon Onion Powder
1 cup Sun-Dried Tomatoes, soaked
1 teaspoon Sea Salt
3 cups **Sun-Dried Tomato Sauce**, recipe page **134**.

Pecans
Contain iron, calcium, phosphorous, and potassium. Should be refrigerated for 1 to 2 months if not consumed immediately because they are highly perishable.

Grind Pecans in food processor until fine. In a bowl, mix pecans with vegetables, spices, and 1 cup of tomato sauce. Shape into loaf and spread tomato sauce on top. Decorate with fresh parsley, celery leaves, sliced olives or pecan halves.

Serves 8

Flax-Sesame Loaf

Dry Mixture:
2 cups Flax Seeds, ground
1 medium Red Bell Pepper, diced
½ medium Red Onion, sliced lengthwise
1 handful Celery Leaves, finely chopped
1 bunch Scallions (Green Onions), chopped
4 heaping tablespoons Sumac
2 tablespoons Dried Parsley
1 teaspoon Basil

Wet ingredients:
½ cup Carrot Juice
1 sprig fresh Parsley
1 stalk Celery and leaves
1 Lettuce leaf, chopped

> **Flax Seeds**
> *Anticancer, antibacterial, and antifungal. Has laxative properties. Flax seed oil is the richest source of Omega-3 Fatty acids of any food. Omega-3 fatty acids are critical for brain function and structure.*

In a bowl, mix dry ingredients. Blend wet ingredients at medium speed. In a bowl, gradually add ½ wet mixture to dry mixture. Shape into a loaf. Use remaining sauce as loaf topping. Decorate with celery leaves, parsley, carrot curls or thinly sliced tomatoes.

House of Mahneel

Serves 8

Battered Mushrooms

8-ounces Button Mushrooms, sliced
Nama shoyu

Wet Batter:
2 cups Wheatberries, sprouted 1 day
1 cup Nutritional Yeast
1/4 cup Flax Seeds, ground
1/2 teaspoon Sea Salt
1 cup Purified Water

Dry Batter:
1 cup Nutritional Yeast
1 cup Wheat Germ
1 tablepoon Garlic Granules
1 tablespoon dried Basil
1/2 teaspoon Sea Salt

Marinate mushrooms in nama shoyu for a few minutes. Blend wet batter ingredients. In a separate bowl, mix dry batter ingredients. Dip mushrooms into wet batter and roll in dry batter and set aside. A faster method is to pour dry ingredients in a sturdy plastic bag, add mushrooms dipped in wet batter, close bag and shake to coat evenly. Place mushrooms on mesh rack of dehydrator and dry at 105 degrees for 4 hours. Flip mushrooms and dry for another 4 hours.

Serves 4

Creamed Corn

4 ears fresh Corn on the Cob
1 tablespoon Maple Syrup
1 teaspoon Dulse
1 dash Cayenne Pepper

Thinly slice corn off cob in layers. Mix with remaining ingredients.

Serves 6

Zvenah Eshet Sar Elyahshuv

Candied Yams

4 small Yams, thinly sliced rounds using mandolin
¼ cup Sesame Oil, cold pressed
1/8 teaspoon freshly grated Nutmeg
¼ teaspoon Cinnamon
1/8 teaspoon Vanilla Bean Seeds
1 medium Orange, juiced
1 teaspoon Orange Peel, ground
½ cup Maple Syrup

Marinate yams in remaining ingredients for at least 8 hours. Stir and serve.

Serves 8 to 10

Zvenah Eshet Sar Elyahshuv

Raw "Collard Greens"

16-ounces Wakame Seaweed
1 small Onion, chopped
1 large Tomato, chopped
2 Garlic Cloves, sliced
¼ cup Nutritional Yeast
1 tablespoon Granulated Garlic
2 teaspoons Onion Powder

Chop seaweed in food processor using slicer blade. Soak for 1 hour and drain. Add remaining ingredients.

Serves 8

Cauliflower Salad

1 small head of Cauliflower, chopped
2 tablespoons Nutritional Yeast
1 tablespoon Granulated Garlic
1 tablespoon Extra Virgin Olive Oil
1 tablespoon Liquid Aminos
1 ½ teaspoons Paprika

Mix together all ingredients. Sprinkle with dulse seaweed flakes and serve.

Serves 6

Mashed "Potatoes"

2 ripe Plantains, mashed with a fork

Enjoy!

Serves 4

Live Potato Salad

1 Jicama, peeled & cubed
1 Red or Yellow Pepper, chopped fine
1 Red Onion, chopped fine
1 Stalk Celery, chopped fine or 1 teaspoon Celery Seeds
Nut Mayo, recipe page **136**
¼ cup Nutritional Yeast
1 tablespoon Granulated Garlic
¼ cup Relish
1 teaspoon Turmeric for color

Mix and serve immediately.

Serves 4

> ### *Jicama*
> *Jicama, (pronounced "HEE-kuh-muh") also known as a Mexican turnip or yam bean, is grown for the large tuberous roots which can be eaten raw. A great source of vitamin C and potassium. The jicama plant is a vine which grows to a length of 20 feet or more. The roots are light brown in color, and may weigh up to 50 pounds.*

Coleslaw

¼ head Green Cabbage, shredded
¼ head Purple Cabbage, shredded
2 Carrots, shredded
½ cup **Nut Mayo**, recipe page **136**.
½ cup Relish (no sugar)
¼ cup Extra Virgin Olive Oil
¼ cup Nutritional Yeast
1 tablespoon Maple Syrup
1 tablespoon Garlic Powder
2 teaspoons Celery Seeds

Mix and serve.

Serves 8

Cabbage
*Alleviates ulcers,
abdominal spasms,
constipation, depression,
and irritability. A good
blood purifier.*

West African

Jollof Rice

2 cups Whole Grain Brown Rice (Sprouted 5-7 days)
1 Red Bell Pepper, diced fine
1 Red Onion, diced fine
1 cup Shredded Carrots
½ cup fresh Green Peas
3 Scallions (Spring Onions)
2 Garlic Cloves, chopped

Sauce:
1 cup Sun-Dried Tomatoes, soaked
3 medium Tomatoes, seeded and diced
2 Tablespoons Extra Virgin Olive Oil
2 Tablespoons Maple Syrup
1 teaspoon Thyme
1 teaspoon Cinnamon
½ teaspoon Cayenne Pepper
¼ cup Nama Shoyu

Mix rice and vegetables. Mix sauce ingredients in a food processor and add to mixture. Marinate for 8 hours and serve.

Serves 4

"Egushi" Greens

1 bunch Mustard Greens, finely chopped
¼ cup Extra Virgin Olive Oil
½ small ripe Tomato, diced
1 Garlic Clove
2 tablespoons Liquid Aminos
½ cup Pumpkin Seeds, soaked overnight
¼ teaspoon Paprika

Egushi seeds are actually lightly colored seeds from a cucumber or melon plant native to Africa.

Blend all ingredients except mustard greens. Pour sauce on greens, mix well, and marinate for 1 hour. Note: if using different greens for this recipe, add a dash of cayenne pepper.

Serves 4

Plantain (Kele-Wele)

2 ripe Plantains, peeled and sliced
¼ cup Coconut Milk
1 Garlic Clove or 1 tablespoon Garlic Granules
1 Scallion (Spring Onion), chopped
2 tablespoons fresh Ginger, grated
½ teaspoon Cayenne Pepper

Mix well and serve.

Serves 4

Ground Nut Stew

¼ cup Carrots, shredded
¼ cup Celery, finely sliced
½ Red Onion, finely chopped
1 ear Corn, cut kernels off cob
1/4 cup Eggplant, peeled, small cubes
½ cup Okra, sliced
2 Tomatoes, diced
Nama Shoyu to taste

Sauce:
1 cup Purified Water
1 cup Raw Peanut Butter
½ cup Maple Syrup
3 tablespoons **Vegetable Seasoning**, recipe page **130**
1 tablespoon Cumin
2 Garlic Cloves, crushed
¼ teaspoon Cayenne

Blend sauce ingredients. Mix vegetables with nama shoyu and add sauce. Serve over soaked seasoned bulgur or sprouted brown rice.

Serves 4

Ground Nut Stew
Groundnut is the common African word for peanut, and Groundnut Stew or Groundnut Chop is one of many Chop dishes; the Western African version is eaten all over sub-Saharan Africa. The Western African style is usually more elaborate, with more ingredients and garnishes. This live version is far healthier.

Nut Patties

1 cup Almonds, soaked 6 to 8 hours, chopped
1 cup Sunflower Seeds, ground
1 Red Bell Pepper, finely chopped
1 Red Onion, finely chopped
1 tablespoon granulated Garlic
1 tablespoon Sage
1 tablespoon Coriander
1 tablespoon Cumin
2 teaspoons Sea Salt

In a bowl, combine all ingredients and mix well. Place in a dehydrator at 100 degrees for 5 hours. Flip onto mesh rack and dehydrate for an additional 3 hours.

Serves 4

Divine Squash Salad

1 small Zucchini, thinly sliced cross-wise
1 small Yellow Squash, thinly sliced cross-wise
1 small Red Onion, thinly sliced
1 Green Chile, chopped
2 tablespoons Extra Virgin Olive Oil
2 tablespoons Nama Shoyu
1 tablespoon grated Ginger
2 teaspoons fresh Lemon Juice
1/8 teaspoon Cayenne Pepper to taste

Mix and serve.

Serves 4

Asian

Tofu-Arame Salad

1 block Tofu, cubed
¼ cup Arame Seaweed, soaked and drained
1 Tablespoon Granulated Kelp
2 Spring Onions, chopped
Liquid Aminos to taste

Gently mix all ingredients and serve.

Serves 4

Sun-Fired Rice

2 cups Whole Grain Brown Rice, soaked & sprouted 5-7 days
½ cup Millet, soaked
½ cup Peas
½ cup Carrots, diced
½ cup Mung Bean Sprouts
¼ cup Nama Shoyu
1 tablespoon Vegetable Seasoning, recipe page **131**.
¼ cup Sesame Oil
2 teaspoons fresh Lime Juice

Mix thoroughly and allow to marinate for one hour before serving.

Serves 4

Live Spring Rolls

1 medium head Green Cabbage, finely shredded
3 Carrots, shredded
2 cups Mushrooms, thinly sliced
1 Red Bell Pepper, thinly sliced
½ small Red Onion, thinly sliced
1-inch piece Ginger Root, peeled & grated
1 Garlic Clove, minced
½ cup Sesame Oil
¼ cup Nama Shoyu
1 pack dry Rice Paper Wraps

In a bowl, thoroughly mix all ingredients except rice wraps. Soak 1 Rice wrap at a time in a plate of warm water for about 30 seconds until it softens. Gently remove from plate, allowing wrap to drain and lie on a flat surface. Spoon out some of the vegetable mixture, squeezing out excess liquid and place in center of wrap. Shape into a log. Wrap by folding one end of wrap over mixture and gently tuck over the long side of the log. Fold the two sides of the wrap over the log. Finally, roll wrap towards the open end. Allow wrap to sit on seam so it will be sealed closed. Serve with **Dipping Sauce**, **Sweet & Sour Sauce**, or **Maple Mustard Sauce**.

Makes about 24 rolls

The Art of Sushi

4 Nori sheets
2 Avocados, peeled, pitted, sliced into sticks
1 Cucumber, peeled, sliced into sticks
1 Red Bell Pepper, thinly sliced

Almond filling:
2 cups Almonds, soaked, pushed through a Champion Juicer or homogenizer.
1 Lemon, juiced
2 teaspoons Kelp

Carrot filling:
2 cups Carrot Pulp
¼ cup Extra Virgin Olive Oil
2 teaspoons granulated Garlic
2 teaspoons Onion Powder
1 tablespoon Maple Syrup
½ teaspoon Sea Salt

> ***Don't get discouraged***
> *Some chefs train for several years at culinary schools in the art of sushi rolling, so if your sushi does not look like those in food magazines and Japanese restaurants, then just keep at it. Practice makes perfect.*

How to Roll:
Mix ingredients for almond filling. In a separate bowl mix carrot filling ingredients. Lay a nori sheet on a sushi mat, shiny side down. Place a line of ½ cup of carrot mixture in the middle of the nori sheet from end to end. Line up slices of avocado, cucumber, and pepper in the center of the carrot to each end. Cover carrot and vegetables with a line of ½ cup of almond mixture. Using a sushi mat, gently roll both edges of the nori sheet over the mixture. Press mat firmly around roll for about 30 seconds to shape it. Remove mat. Seal closed with a little water and rest roll on the seam for a few minutes allowing mixture to moisten the nori sheet. Using a wet, sharp knife , begin by cutting the roll in half, and each half in half until you have eight 1 ½-inch rounds. Wipe knife with a damp cloth after each cut. Serve with Hot & Spicy dipping sauce.

Makes 32 rolls

Stir-Live

8-ounce pack Bean Thread Noodles
1 small Red Bell Pepper, sliced thin
1 small Yellow Bell Pepper, sliced thin
1 small Red Onion, sliced thin
3 ounces Mushrooms, sliced
1 Tablespoon fresh Ginger root, peeled & grated
1 handful Mung Bean Sprouts
1 Lemon, juiced
¼ cup cold-pressed Sesame Oil
½ cup Maple Syrup
1 tablespoon fresh Garlic, pressed
½ teaspoon Kelp Powder
¼ cup Liquid Aminos

Boil water and remove from the flame. Immediately soak bean thread noodles until soft and tender. Drain in a colander and rinse with cold water. In a bowl, combine vegetables: Peppers, Onions, Mushrooms, and Mung Bean Sprouts. Set aside. In a blender, combine ginger root, lemon juice, sesame oil, maple syrup, garlic, kelp and liquid aminos. Blend at medium speed. Transfer noodles to a separate bowl and pour blended mixture over noodles. Add vegetables. Mix thoroughly and allow a few hours to marinate. Eat with chopsticks.

Serves 8

Seaweed Salad

2 cups dried Wakame Seaweed
1 Red Onion, diced
1 medium Tomato, diced
½ cup Black Olives, pitted & sliced
2 tablespoons Garlic Granules
¼ cup cold-presses Sesame Oil
Sea Salt (optional)
Dash of Cayenne Pepper

Chop seaweed in food processor using slicer blade. Soak seaweed for approximately 10 minutes. Drain. Mix remaining ingredients. Add sea salt only if seaweed brand does not have a natural salty taste.

Serves 8

Wakame Eggplant Salad

1 Large Eggplant, peeled & diced
1 ounce rehydrated Wakame Seaweed
1 cup **Tahini Dressing**, see page **135**
1 cup Mushrooms, chopped
2 cloves Garlic, pressed
1 tablespoon granulated Kelp

Mix well, chill and serve.

Serves 6

House of Mahneel

> ***Eggplants***
> *A cooling watery fruit good for the blood. When purchasing, buy young smaller eggplants which will be firm, unbruised, brightly colored and not bitter.*

Chinese Cabbage

1 head small Chinese Cabbage, shredded
1 Orange, juiced
1 Lemon, juiced
1 tablespoon untoasted Sesame Oil
1 tablespoon Flax Seed Oil
2 Garlic Cloves, crushed
2 teaspoons unhulled Sesame Seeds
1 teaspoon Orange Zest, ground
1 tablespoon Nama Shoyu
1 tablespoon Agave Nectar
1 tablespoon fresh Ginger Root, peeled and grated
1/8 teaspoon Cayenne Pepper

Mix all ingredients. Marinate for one hour and serve.

Serves 8

Nori Dim Sum

1 Avocado, pitted, peeled, and mashed
Nori sheets, cut a nori sheet into fourths

Place a tablespoon of mixture in center of each Nori Sheet. Bring 4 corners together and gently press down into a floret. Use a little water to keep ends together.

Thai Sober Noodles

1 large Zucchini
1 large Yellow Squash
1 Red Pepper, sliced thin
1 Carrot, shredded
½ small Red Onion, thinly sliced
¼ cup Broccoli Florets, chopped fine
½ cup Mung Bean Sprouts
¼ cup Fresh Basil Leaves
1 Garlic Clove, crushed
¼ cup tablespoons Flax Seed Oil
2 tablespoons **Vegetable Seasoning,**
    recipe page **131**.
2 tablespoons Nama Shoyu
2 tablespoons Maple Syrup

With a potato peeler, cut zucchini, yellow
squash, and carrot into long thin strips. These
will serve as your noodles. Add remaining vegetables and mix thoroughly. In a separate
bowl, mix flax seed oil, vegetable seasoning, nama shoyu and maple syrup. Mix with
vegetables. For better results, allow to marinate for at least one hour before serving.

Serves 8

Eggplant with Garlic Sauce

1 Eggplant, peeled & cut into very thin triangles

Garlic Sauce:
¼ cup Sesame Oil
2 Garlic cloves
1-inch piece Fresh Ginger Root, peeled
¼ cup Tamari or Nama Shoyu
2 tablespoons Maple Syrup
1 teaspoon Arrowroot powder

Marinate eggplant in salt water for 30 minutes. Rinse and pat dry. Blend garlic sauce ingredients. Mix with eggplant. Allow to marinate for 1 hour.

Serves 2

Harmony Spinach

1 bunch Spinach
¼ cup Untoasted Sesame Oil
1 tablespoon Ginger, peeled and grated
2 Garlic Cloves, minced
2 tablespoons Maple Syrup
2 tablespoons Liquid Aminos

Wash spinach thoroughly, remove stems and chop. Mix ingredients and serve.

Serves 4

Latin

Guacamole

1 Avocado, peeled and pitted
¼ teaspoon Sea Salt
1 small Tomato, diced
¼ medium Red Onion, chopped
Juice of 1 Lemon

Mash avocado with sea salt. Add tomatoes, lemon juice and onions. Place the avocado seed in guacamole to maintain color. Best if eaten immediately.

Serves 2

Taco Salad

2 cups Bulgur Wheat, soaked overnight
2 Tomatoes, diced
1 cup **Sunshine Cheese**, recipe page **136**
½ cup Brown Olives, pitted and sliced
1 head Romaine Lettuce, shredded
½ Red Onion, diced
2 teaspoons Sage
1 tablespoon granulated Garlic
1 teaspoon Sea Salt
Tortilla Chips, recipe page **104**

Mix Bulgur with sage, garlic, and sea salt. Layer Tortilla Chips, shredded lettuce, 1 scoop of bulgur mixture, encircle with tomatoes, top with olives, onions and cheese. Sprinkle with dried parsley or paprika to decorate.

Serves 4

Nut Chili

1 cup Walnuts or Brazil Nuts, chopped fine
5 medium Tomatoes, diced
1 handful Celery leaves, chopped
1 Onion, diced
3 Garlic cloves, minced
2 tablespoons fresh Fennel, chopped
2 teaspoons dried Onion
1 teaspoon Dulse Seaweed flakes
Cumin to taste

Mix ingredients together.

Serves 4

House of Mahneel

Helpful Hint
To remove stains from food processing equipment, apply a paste of 2 tablespoons baking soda to 1 tablespoon water. Let stand overnight. Rinse and dry.

Mushroom Fajitas

1 Red Pepper, seeds removed, thinly sliced
1 Yellow Pepper, seeds removed, thinly sliced
1 Red Onion, thinly sliced
4 Portabello Mushrooms, stems removed, sliced
¼ cup Olive Oil
1 teaspoon Sage
1 teaspoon Basil
1 tablespoon Garlic Granules
4 tablespoons Liquid Aminos
Tortilla Wraps or wraps of your choice, see page **40**.

Marinate peppers, onions, and mushrooms in olive oil sage, basil, garlic, and liquid aminos for 30 minutes. Wrap vegetables in the wrap of your choice.

Serves 4

Jicama

1 large Jicama, peeled and sliced
Juice of 1 Lime
½ teaspoon Sea Salt
1/8 teaspoon Cayenne Pepper

Mix well and serve.

Burritos

Home-made Matzos or Lettuce Leaf
1 Avocado, peeled, pitted, mashed
1 small Tomato, chopped
½ cup Brown Olives, pitted
1 tablespoon Lemon Juice
Cayenne Pepper to taste
Sea Salt to taste

Mix vegetables and seasonings.
Wrap in matzos. Muy Bien!

Serves 4

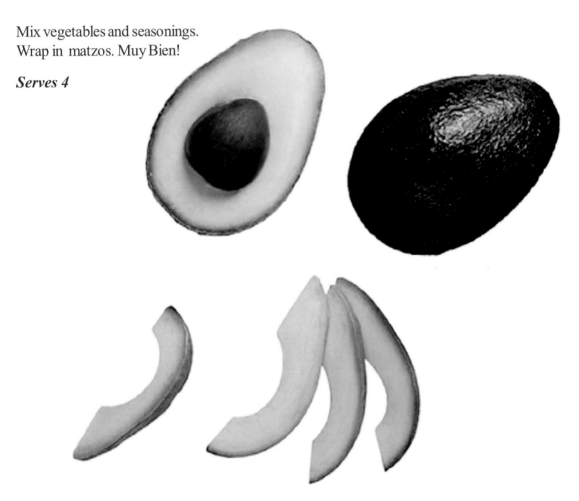

Salsa

4 Roma Tomatoes, seeded and chopped
1 cup Sun-Dried Tomatoes, soaked
1 Jalapeno Pepper, seeded and chopped
2 Garlic Cloves, peeled and chopped
¼ cup Brown Olives, pitted & sliced

Drain Sun Dried Tomatoes and chop in food processor. Combine all ingredients together in a bowl.

Makes 1 ½ cups

Tortilla Chips

2 cups fresh Yellow Sweet Corn, cut from cob
3 tablespoons Golden Flax Seeds, ground
1 cup Sunflower Seeds, soaked
¼ cup Olive Oil
¼ cup Yellow Onion, chopped
1 large Garlic clove, minced
1 tablespoon fresh Lemon Juice
1 teaspoon Sea Salt
1 teaspoon Poppy Seeds
1/8 teaspoon Cumin Powder
1/8 teaspoon Nutmeg
½ Cup Purified Water

Mix all ingredients in a food processor until smooth. Spread a thin layer on teflex sheet of dehydrator. Dehydrate at 105-degrees for 4 hours. Flip over, remove from dehydrator, cut into triangles, and dehydrate on mesh sheet for 12 hours or until crisp.

Mediterranean

Living Hummus

2 cups Sprouted Chickpeas (Garbanzo beans)
1 cup Purified Water
¼ cup Olive Oil
¼ cup Tahini
¼ cup Fresh Lemon Juice
4 Cloves fresh Garlic, pressed
¼ cup Parsley
1 teaspoon Sea Salt
¼ teaspoon Cayenne Pepper

Chop sprouted chickpeas in a food processor using the s-blade. Gradually pour in water until it forms a smooth paste. Pour into a bowl and mix with remaining ingredients- carefully keeping the mixture firm. Decorate with a slice of lemon and fresh or dried parsley. Eat with celery sticks, crackers or nori sheets.

Serves 8

House of Mahneel

Chickpeas
Good for pancreas, heart and stomach. High in vitamin C and iron.

Judean Tabbouleh

½ cup Bulgur wheat, soaked overnight in 2 cups of water
2 medium Tomatoes, peeled, seeded, chopped fine, drained
2 cups Fresh Parsley, finely chopped
7 Scallions, finely chopped
½ cup Mint Leaves
¼ cup Extra Virgin Olive Oil
1 Lemon, juiced
2 teaspoons Cumin
2 teaspoons Sage
1 teaspoon Sea Salt
1/8 teaspoon Cayenne Pepper

Mix all ingredients. B'tayah-vone! (To your health)

Serves 4

Stuffed Grape Leaves

8 ounces Grape Leaves

2 cups **Judean Tabbouleh**, recipe above with these adjustments:
2 cups Bulgur Wheat
1 cup Parsley
1 tablespoon Sage
2 teaspoons Sea Salt

Grape leaves can be purchased from Mediterranean, Latino, and gourmet markets

Drain Bulgar. Lay 1 grape leaf on a clean, flat, and dry surface with the stem facing you. Spoon 2 tablespoons of Taboulleh onto the center of the leaf. Begin rolling from the leaf base, folding in the sides to enclose the filling. Continue rolling and rest the roll on the seam to seal.

Makes about 25 rolls

Baba Ganoush

2 large Eggplants, peeled & finely diced
¼ cup Tahini
1 small Red Onion, chopped
7 Garlic Cloves, peeled & crushed
1 tablespoon ground Cumin
1 teaspoon ground Coriander
2 tablespoons fresh Lemon Juice
1 tablespoon Olive Oil
1 teaspoon Sea Salt
Paprika or Dried Parsley to garnish

Chopping Onions without Shedding a Tear
(So they say)

- Burn a candle
- Hold a wooden match stick in your mouth
- Use a sharp knife
- Peel under running water
- Refrigerate before cutting
- Trim the root last

Blend ingredients except for eggplant and garnishes. In a bowl combine eggplant and blended ingredients and mix well. Decorate with Paprika or Dried Parsley.

Rawlafels

½ Pound Almonds, ground
2 tablespoons Coriander
2 tablespoons Kelp
1 ½ tablespoons Granulated Garlic
1 ½ tablespoons Cumin
1 tablespoon Nutritional Yeast
1 tablespoon Paprika
1 tablespoon dried Onion
1-2 tablespoons Extra Virgin Olive Oil

Combine all ingredients and mix well. Add purified water until mixture has a dough-like consistency. Form into balls. Serve on nori sheets or matzo with **Tahini Dressing** and diced cucumbers and tomatoes.

Makes approximately 14 balls

Hecumliel HaCohane

Vegetable Kebobs

1 Red Pepper, chopped in 1-inch squares
1 Green Pepper, chopped in 1-inch squares
1 Red Onion, chopped in 1-inch squares
1 pint small Button Mushrooms
1 Small, Young Eggplant, peeled, chopped into medium cubes
8 ounces Cherry Tomatoes
Skewer Sticks

Marinade:
½ cup Tamari
¼ cup Maple Syrup
¼ cup Cold Pressed Sesame Oil
1 tablespoon Fresh Lemon Juice
1 tablespoon Garlic Granules

Alternate putting a piece of each vegetable on to stick. Allow kebobs to marinate for at least 1 hour before serving. The longer the marinading time, the tastier the kebob.

Serves 10

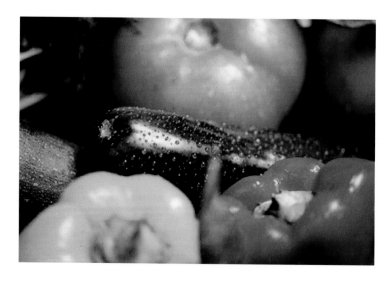

Rice Salad

2 cups Whole Grain Brown Rice, sprouted 5 days
Juice of Fresh Lemon
Grated Lemon Rind
1 tablespoon Olive Oil
1 tablespoon Dill Weed
4 Green Onions (Scallions), chopped fine
1 cup Fresh Parsley, chopped
¼ cup Nama Shoyu
½ cup soaked Dates, pitted and chopped
¼ cup Cashew Pieces, soaked

Combine all ingredients and mix well. Best served after refrigerating.

Serves 4

Olive Pate

12 ounces Brown Olives, pitted
½ small Red Onion, finely chopped
2 tablespoons Capers
2 tablespoons Fresh Lemon Juice
½ teaspoon Thyme

Black Olives are sometimes treated with dye, so we use brown olives instead.

Blend all ingredients.

Makes 1 ½ cups

Eggplant with Pesto and Tomato Sauce

1 medium Eggplant, peeled, thinly sliced length-wise
¼ cup Nama Shoyu

Pesto:
7 leaves fresh Basil, chopped fine
1/3 cup Extra Virgin Olive Oil
¼ cup Pine Nuts
2 Garlic Cloves
½ teaspoon Sea Salt

Sun-Dried Tomato Sauce, recipe page **134**

Mix pesto ingredients. Marinate eggplant in nama shoyu for 10 minutes. Add pesto. Top with sun-dried tomato sauce.

Cucumber-Tomato Salad

2 Cucumbers, peeled and sliced
2 ripe Tomatoes, halved and sliced
3 tablespoons Olive Oil
2 tablespoons Lemon Juice
1 tablespoons Nama Shoyu
1 tablespoon Dill
½ teaspoon dried Basil
½ teaspoon dried Oregano
½ teaspoon dried Thyme

Mix all ingredients thoroughly. Be-vra-kah!

Serves 4

Caribbean

Tomato Rice

2 cups Bulghur, soaked 4 to 6 hours
2 cups **Sun-Dried Tomato Sauce**, recipe page **134**.
2 teaspoons Extra Virgin Olive Oil
½ cup Red Onion, chopped fine
2 Garlic Cloves, peeled & crushed
¼ cup **Vegetable Seasoning**, recipe page **131**.
¼ teaspoon Sea Salt
1/8 teaspoon Cayenne Pepper
1/8 teaspoon dried Thyme

Combine all ingredients. Allow to marinate for 4 hours.

Serves 6

Jerk Tofu

1 block Tofu, cubed
½ cup Tamari
1 Yellow Bell Pepper, thinly sliced
1 Red Bell Pepper, thinly sliced
1 small Red Onions, peeled and thinly sliced
2 tablespoons Extra Virgin Olive Oil
2 tablespoons of **Jerk Seasoning**, recipe page **130**.

Marinate tofu cubes in tamari for 30 minutes. Drain and add remaining ingredients.

Serves 4

Peppered Portabello Mushrooms

2 Portabello Mushrooms, sliced
2 Scallions, chopped
2 Garlic Cloves, crushed
1 teaspoon Thyme
¼ cup Extra Virgin Olive Oil
¼ cup **Vegetable Seasoning**, recipe page **131**.
1 teaspoon powdered Kelp
1 teaspoon Dulse Flakes
1 teaspoon Cayenne Pepper
1 teaspoon Sea Salt

Marinate Mushrooms in tamari for 30 minutes. Drain and add remaining ingredients.

Serves 4

Jamaican Delight

2 Ripe Plantains, peeled and sliced
½ cup Sun-Dried Tomatoes, soaked and chopped
½ cup Black Olives, pitted and sliced
2 Scallions (Green Onions)
¼ cup Extra Virgin Olive Oil
1 tablespoon Liquid Aminos
1 tablespoon fresh Lime Juice
½ teaspoon Cayenne Pepper (optional)

Mix all ingredients.

Serves 4

Ripe Plantain
Choose plantain that is yellow with black spots and should have the firmness of a banana. Avoid plantain that is too soft or has broken skin. Do not store in refrigerator until after it is peeled.

Curried Okra

2 cups fresh Okra, sliced
1 small Red Onion, thinly sliced
2 Garlic Cloves, crushed
2 tablespoons Extra Virgin Olive Oil
1 teaspoon Onion Powder
1 teaspoon Coriander
½ teaspoon **Curry Powder**, see recipe page **132**
½ teaspoon Thyme
1/8 teaspoon Cayenne Pepper
Liquid Aminos to taste

Okra
Contains B-complex
vitamins and vitamin C
Good for your stomach.
Alleviates constipation.
Purchase smaller, softer
pods for your live meal.

Blend garlic with olive oil. Combine remaining ingredients in a bowl and mix well. Add garlic and olive oil mixture.

Serves 2

Ben Tsedek Ben Baruch

Chickpea Roti

2 cups Sprouted Chickpeas
1 Jicama, peeled chop into ¼-inch cubes
½ cup Shredded Cabbage
1 Red Onion, peeled and diced
¼ cup Olive Oil
2 tablespoons Fresh Ginger Root, peeled and grated
4 teaspoons **Curry Powder**, see recipe page **132**
2 teaspoons Sea Salt
1 teaspoon Cayenne Pepper
Tortilla wrap, matzo, or your favorite wrap, see page **40**

Place sprouted chickpeas in a food processor until creamy. Add water if necessary. Combine all ingredients and marinate for 4 hours. Scoop into your favorite wrap and fold it closed. Enjoy.

Serves 6

Desserts

Carob Sauce

½ cup Raw Carob Powder
1 cup Molasses

Mix and serve over your favorite dessert.

Makes 1 ½ cups

Tahini Sauce

3/4 cup Tahini
¼ cup Water
¼ cup Maple Syrup

Blend. Add to your favorite dessert.

Makes 1 cup

Strawberry Sauce

1 cup fresh Strawberries
¼ cup Maple Syrup or Agave Nectar

Blend. Refrigerate for 1 hour. Serve over Real Live Cheesecake or Fruit Parfait.

Makes 1 cup

Orange Bundt Cake

4 cups Dates, pitted
3 cups Walnuts, soaked and drained
2 cups Shredded Coconut, ground in coffee grinder
½ cup Sesame Seeds, ground in coffee grinder
2 tablespoons dried Orange Peel, ground
1 teaspoon pure Orange Extract

Icing:
1 cup Maple Syrup
1½ cups Tahini
1 teaspoon Orange Juice

"PITTED" DATES
Always rinse dates and check each one for pits, insect eggs and debris, even if they are "pitted." In my early days of eating raw, I was very unfamiliar with dates. In an attempt to make a live pie, I opened a package of dates, threw one in the juicer, and destroyed a perfectly good $200 champion juicer...that belonged to my boss.

Chop walnuts in food processor with S-blade until fine. Remove and set aside. Chop dates in food processor with S-blade until consistency becomes a paste. Add coconut and sesame seeds to walnuts and mix thoroughly. Add orange peel and orange flavor to processed dates. Press date mixture into walnut mixture until it holds together. Press into a bundt cake pan and place in freezer for an hour or so. Blend icing ingredients and set aside. Remove cake from pan (do never use a metal knife, they are known for destroying cake pans). Drizzle on icing. Decorate with freshly peeled orange rind and slices. The cake will last in the freezer or refrigerator for a month or longer, but don't wait too long!. Be sure to remove decorations if storing beyond 2 days.

Serves 12

Fruity Ice Cream

3 Mangos, peeled and diced
2 Bananas, Peeled
1 cup Sliced Strawberries

Freeze fruit at least for 5 hours. Press each fruit separately through a champion juicer or a homogenizer. Serve immediately.

Serves 2

Date Coconut Bars

½ cup Dates, pitted
¼ cup Coconut, shredded
¼ cup Sunflower Seeds

Grind sunflower seeds and shredded coconut in a seed grinder separately. Process dates in food processor using the s-blade until they form a ball or a paste. In a separate bowl, mix together all ingredients. Press into a pan. Refrigerate for at least 2 hours. Cut into 2-inch squares.

Makes about 12 bars

Bilgah Baht Israel

Real Live Cashew Cheesecake

3 cups Cashews, soaked
3/4 cup Dates, pitted
½ cup Fresh Coconut
3 Lemons, juiced
Purified Water

Crust:
20 Dates, pitted
1 cup Almonds

Grind crust almonds into a powder in a food processor. Add pitted dates and grind into a grainy texture. Press mixture into a pie dish. Grind cashews, dates, coconut oil, and lemon juice in food processor, slowly adding a little water until it has a firm and creamy texture. Spoon mixture into pie dish. Top with a slice of lemon, a drizzle of strawberry sauce, or zig-zag with carob sauce.

Serves 8

Sesame Balls

1 cup Sesame Seeds, ground
½ cup Sunflower Seeds, ground
10 Dates, pitted
1 teaspoon fresh Lemon Juice
¼ teaspoon Vanilla

Sesame Seeds, whole, unhulled, soaked

Grind dates in a food processor and mix with remaining ingredients. Shape into balls. Roll in whole sesame seeds.

Makes about a dozen balls

Apple Pie

5 Fuji Apples, peeled and cored
1 cup Dark Agave Nectar
1 teaspoon Cinnamon
1 teaspoon Nutmeg
3 tablespoons Agar Agar Sea Vegetable
1 Cup Purified Water

Crust:
2 cups Walnuts, chopped
1 cup Dates, pitted
¼ cup Sesame Seeds, ground
¼ cup Coconut, shredded

Stevia Conversion Chart	
SUGAR	STEVIA
2 tsp	½ tsp
1/4 cup	3 tsp
1/3 cup	4 tsp
1/2 cup	6 tsp
3/4 cup	9 tsp
1 cup	12 tsp
2 cups	24 tsp

To make crust. Process walnuts and dates separately in food processor using the s-blade. Mix walnuts, dates, sesame seeds, and coconut together in a bowl and press crust into round 9-inch pan including the sides. For pie filling, boil water and remove from flame. Stir in agar agar to dissolve and allow to cool- use before completely cool because it will become solid at room temperature. Slice apples in food processor using the slicer blade. In a bowl, gently mix apples, cinnamon, nutmeg, agar agar and agave sweetener. Fill pie crust with apple mixture. Refrigerate for at least thirty minutes.

Serves 8

Sweet Potato Pie

3 Sweet Potatoes, chopped
1 cup purified Water
1 cup Maple Syrup
1 tablespoon Cinnamon
1 tablespoon Nutmeg
1 teaspoon Vanilla

Crust, see **Apple Pie** recipe page **123**.

Press crust ingredients into a round 9-inch pie dish. Blend remaining ingredients in a high-speed blender until mixture forms a smooth paste. Fill crust.

Serves 8

Sweet Potato or Yam?

Sweet potatoes and yams are two different vegetables. A sweet potato is actually a weed that is sweeter in taste, high in vitamins A and C, and good for kidneys and the stomach. Yams are a more starchy tuber and have medicinal properties that are beneficial for a woman's reproductive system. They also bind with heavy metals and assist with their detoxification.

Carob-Mint Sandwich Cookies

2 cups Walnuts
3/4 cup Dates, pitted
¼ cup Raw Carob Powder
2 tablespoons Molasses

Filling:
½ cup Tahini
10 Dates, pitted
1 tablespoon fresh Mint leaves, chopped or ½ teaspoon Mint extract
¼ teaspoon Spirulina
Purified Water

Carob is a great chocolate substitute full of calcium without the caffeine. The fresh pods are a wonderful snack.

Grind walnuts fine in a food processor using the S-blade and transfer to a separate bowl. Process dates in the processor until forming a paste. Add to walnuts. Add carob and molasses to the mixture and mix well. Using a tablespoon, scoop out mixture, roll into balls and flatten into circles about 1/8-inch thick and 2-inches in diameter. Dehydrate at 95-degrees for 4 to 6 hours on the screen just to hold their shape. For filling, place all filling ingredients except water in food processor until smooth. Add water if needed. Remove "cookies" from dehydrator, spoon filling on to one wafer and top with another wafer. Serve to children of all ages.

Makes approximately 15 cookies

Brownies

1 pound Dates, pitted
1 cup raw Almond Butter
1 cup raw Carob Powder
1/3 cup Maple Syrup

Process dates in food processor using s-blade. In a bowl, mix dates and remaining ingredients. Press into a square pan. Refrigerate for an hour. Cut into squares. Decorate with sliced almonds.

Serves 12

Tropical Parfait

2 large ripe Mangoes, peeled and diced
1 medium Pineapple, peeled and diced
1 large Papaya, peeled, seeded and diced
2 cups Cashews, soaked overnight
¼ cup Dark Agave Nectar
Strawberry slices to decorate

Blend cashews and agave nectar in a high speed blender into a whip cream texture. In a tall clear glass, alternate layers of papaya, cashew whip cream, pineapple, cashew whip, mangoes, cashew whip and decorate with strawberry slices. Refrigerate for at least 1 hour before serving.

Serves 4

Snacks

The blessing of a living diet is the variety of tasty treats that nature has to offer which is both healthy and infinite.

Fresh Fruit

Mangoes, Bananas, Grapes, Apples, Pears, Oranges, Grapefruit, Tangerines, Kiwi, Cherries, Strawberries, Blueberries, Raspberries, Blackberries, Goji Berries, Starfruit, Jackfruit, Papaya, Pineapple, Watermelon, Cantaloupe, Honeydew, Peaches, Plums, Pomegranates, Lychee, Dates, Raisins, Tamarind, Figs...

Frozen Fruit

Banana slices - peel ripe bananas, slice, and freeze

Mango cubes - peel, dice and freeze

Nuts & Seeds

Pecans, Pistachios, Walnuts, Almonds, Brazil Nuts, Cashews, Pumpkin Seeds, Sunflower Seeds...

Spice It Up

Salt Substitute

4 tablespoons onion granules
2 tablespoons Stevia
3 teaspoons Brown Mustard Seeds
1 teaspoon Celery Seeds
1 teaspoon Lemon Peel
1 teaspoon Thyme
1 teaspoon Paprika
½ teaspoon Chili Powder

Fill empty spice bottles with your favorite combinations. They are great to travel with.

Grind celery seeds, brown mustard seeds, and lemon peel in coffee or seed grinder. Transfer to a bowl and add remaining ingredients. Mix well. Store in a spice container in a cool dry place.

Makes ½ cup

Jerk Seasoning

1 tablespoon Chili pepper
1 tablespoon ground Thyme
1 tablespoon Allspice
2 teaspoons Green Stevia
2 teaspoons Sea Salt
1 teaspoon ground Onion flakes
1 teaspoon ground Nutmeg
1 teaspoon ground Cinnamon

Mix ingredients.

Makes about 5 tablespoons

Vegetable Seasoning

4 stalks of Celery, finely chopped
1 Zucchini, finely chopped
1 Yellow Squash, finely chopped
2 Carrots, shredded
1 large Yellow Onion, finely chopped
2 cups Spinach, finely chopped
1 Red Bell Pepper, finely chopped
1 handful Mushrooms, finely chopped
2 Roma Tomatoes, finely diced

1 cup Nutritional Yeast
1 teaspoon Sea Salt *(optional)*
1 teaspoon granulated Garlic

Spread a thin layer of all vegetables on mesh racks of dehydrator. Dehydrate at 105 degrees for 12 hours. Place teflex sheet on bottom rack to catch falling pieces. Place dehydrated vegetables in a food processor with nutritional yeast, sea salt and garlic. Grind into a powder. Can be stored in a refrigerator for up to 6 months- but the fresher the better. Add seasonings to salads, sauces, nut loafs, flax crackers, and more.

Makes 2 cups

Hot & Spicy Dipping Sauce

1 cup Tamari
¼ cup untoasted Sesame Oil
1 teaspoon Cayenne Pepper

Blend. Serve with Live Spring Rolls.

Makes 1 ¼ cups

Curry Powder

2 tablespoons Coriander seeds
1 tablespoon Fennel seeds
1 ½ tablespoon Cumin seeds
1 tablespoon Fenugreek seeds
1 tablespoon shredded Coconut
½ teaspoon Brown Mustard seeds

Grind fine in a seed grinder. Must store in refrigerator.

Chinese Five Spice Powder

¼ cup Anise Stars
¼ cup Cinnamon
1 tablespoon Fennel seeds
1 teaspoon Cloves
1 teaspoon Cayenne Pepper

Grind fine in seed grinder. Store in a spice bottle.

Zahtar

2 tablespoon Sesame Seeds, unhulled
2 tablespoons ground Thyme
1 tablespoon ground Sumac

Mix and store in a spice bottle.

Pesto

1/3 cup Pine Nuts (Pignolia Nuts)
2 Garlic Cloves
2 cups Fresh Basil, chopped
¼ cup Extra Virgin Olive Oil
1 teaspoon Sea Salt

Grind pine nuts, garlic, olive oil and salt in a food processor. Transfer to a bowl and mix with basil. Serve pesto on pizza, raw sandwiches, zucchini noodles, or in stuffed tomatoes

Makes 2 cups

Maple Mustard Sauce

¼ cup Brown Mustard Seeds, ground in seed grinder
1 Lemon, juiced
1 Garlic Clove
1 tablespoon Yellow Onion
1 tablespoon Extra Virgin Olive Oil
¼ teaspoon Turmeric Powder
¼ teaspoon Allspice, ground
¼ cup Maple Syrup

Blend and serve with Live Spring Rolls.

Makes 1 cup

Sun-Dried Tomato Sauce

2 cups Sun-dried Tomatoes, soaked, reserve water
4 Roma Tomatoes
2 Garlic Cloves
2 tablespoons Maple Syrup
2 tablespoons Basil
1 teaspoon Oregano
1 teaspoon Thyme
2 teaspoons Red Onion, chopped
2 teaspoons Cumin powder
1 dash Sage powder

Blend ingredients with 1 cup of water from soaked tomatoes. Let sauce sit for 30 minutes to allow water to drain. Water may be used for other recipes.

Makes 3 cups

Tahini Dressing

1 cup Tahini
1 cup Purified Water
1 large Garlic Clove, chopped
¼ cup fresh Parsley, chopped
1 Lemon, juiced

Pour water in blender, add remaining ingredients, and blend. Serve with salad.

Makes 2 cups

Bilgah Baht Israel

Tahini
A high-protein paste made from ground hulled sesame seeds. Tahini is generally made from raw seeds and sesame butter from roasted seeds.

Basil Dressing

1 cup of Extra Virgin Olive Oil
3 Garlic Cloves, pressed
3 tablespoons Apple Cider Vinegar
2 tablespoons Basil
Sea Salt to taste

Blend all ingredients together.

Makes 1 ½ cups

Kanunah B. Israel

Nut Mayo

2 cups Cashews, soaked
½ cup Extra Virgin Olive Oil
1 Lemon, juiced
1 teaspoon Sea Salt
Purified Water

Mix in a food processor or high speed blender. Slowly add a little water until mixture is smooth and creamy.

Makes 2 cups

Sunshine Cheese

2 cups Cashews, soaked
¼ cup Nutritional Yeast
2 Garlic Cloves
1 teaspoon Sea Salt
½ cup Purified Water

Place all ingredients except water in a blender or food processor and mix on high speed. Slowly pour in water until texture becomes creamy. Store in refrigerator. Add more water for a creamier cheese.

Makes 2 cups

Sweet & Sour Sauce

2 Lemons, juiced
½ teaspoon fresh Ginger Root
4 teaspoons Tamari
1 cup ripe Pineapple, peeled and chopped
2 teaspoons Arrow Root Powder

Blend ingredients. Refrigerate for one hour to thicken sauce.

Makes 2 cups

Wild Sesame Dip

2 cups Black Sesame Seeds
2 medium Carrots, chopped
1 large Onion, chopped
3 Cloves Fresh Garlic

Blend all ingredients beginning on the lowest speed, gradually reaching the highest setting until mixture is creamy. If you don't have access to a high speed blender, then grind sesame seeds in a seed grinder and finely chop the vegetables before blending all ingredients together.

Serves 3 to 4

House of Mahneel

Living Testimonies

Many are experiencing the joys of a regenerative diet. Some are prominent figures in the raw food movement and others are ordinary people just like you and me. Although the thoughts and approaches of the interviewees featured here may vary, they have inspirational stories and invaluable techniques to share with the world. They are living proof that living a raw lifestyle is attainable and a great blessing.

Prince Aharon Ben Israel, 64, a leader in the African Hebrew Israelite Community.

Karyn Calabrese, 57, owner of Karyn's Fresh Corner and Inner Beauty Center in Chicago, has been featured on The Oprah Winfrey Show, "Age Defying Women" aired on May 5, 2000.

Amen Khum Ra, 35, an attorney and one of our beloved customers at Everlasting Life Health Food Store in Washington DC.

Annette Larkins, 62, aired a 12-part health series called "Health Alternatives with Living Foods With Annette Larkins" in Miami Florida and is considering syndication for the show.

The Talifero Family hosts a website that includes how to raise raw vegan children and conducts raw food retreats in California.

Migda Baht Yehuda, 33, member of the African Hebrew Israelite Community and studies organic agriculture.

Dr. Aris La Tham, 56, holds a PhD in Food Science. A living foods gourmet chef who has created his own Sunfire Cuisine, hosts raw food retreats in Jamaica.

Artis Eugene Hinson, 59, owns the Body Ecology Attunement Center in North Carolina.

Tolentin Chan, 43, co-owner of Quintessence Raw Food Restaurant with 3 locations in New York.

Lynda Carter, "over 50" nutritional consultant, live foods chef, and owner Alive and Raw Caterers in Richmond VA.

Dr. Llaila Afrika, 58, doctor of naturopathy and author of Afrikan Holistic Health.

Bilgah Baht Israel, living in Israel, has wonderful results with raising her three children on raw.

Zachary Ramzey III, 61, owner of Detox International, a wellness center in Louisiana.

Lillian Butler, 49, owner of Raw Soul Catering business in New York.

Khanunah B Israel, a mother, raw food chef and fashion model residing in Israel.

Dick Gregory, 73, social activist, author, comedian, nutritionist who beat cancer with living foods lifestyle.

PRINCE AHARON BEN ISRAEL - *Age 64*
*Dimona, Israel - **Raw for 20 years***

I thank Yah (God of Israel). I'm not a person who speaks in a mythical realm, instead, I speak about spirituality. I keep things practical because spirituality is very real. It is simply the ability to see and discern Truth. When I came into the knowledge of the Truth, I moved to Israel from Ohio in 1973. At the time, I wore glasses and believed that the raw diet would help to improve my eyesight. I also experienced back problems. I was really inspired by a brother named Nekhemiyah whom I studied with. He started me reading books by Ann Wigmore and Viktoras Kulvinskas' Survival into the 21st Century. Through my studies, I became aware of how Western society is geared more towards vitamins, starches, and protein, protein, protein. I knew this wasn't the best thing to do. I learned that an alkaline diet was best and studied how to get away from proteins.

One of the main things that convinced me was that I used to work and eat late at night, which resulted in sour stomach. I didn't like that. Cooking foods destroys the digestive enzymes. When I eat raw foods, I don't have that problem. I used to love soy ice cream like you wouldn't believe. I would eat it every day if I could. However, starches cause mucous, and, mucous-forming foods are the reason for all sickness. People don't believe this because they go to the doctor and are told all types of things. Learning that made me stop. I haven't eaten any ice cream in over a year. Another challenge for me was eating and drinking at the same time. I'd done it all my life. The thoughts stayed with me for a long time until I finally broke the habit. In 1982, when I was working in Washington, DC, I went through a healing crisis. I started to itch and it drove me crazy. I tried creams, peroxides...nothing worked. This went on for about 3 days. I also had high blood pressure in the 1980s- about 100/140. It's better now- about 70/90.

Everybody is writing books, about diet and nutrition, but these books are more geared towards commercialism because talk about <u>health</u> is talk about <u>life</u>, and, that's not part of the Western construct. Diet has to coincide with a Holy Spirit- the power to refrain from and resist the things that are detrimental. Spirituality has to do with culture. Since culture is the totality of human expressiveness, everything you do is an expression of a holy or unholy spirit. A live diet is the cultural expression of Divinity. When you are cooking, you are taking the live enzymes and killing them; water escapes, and, the nutrients are being taken out of the food. The higher the nutrients in the food, the healthier the body. Everything has to be in alignment with life. You can't say that you are influenced by the Holy Spirit and you are doing things that contradict life. Spiritual elevation can not be achieved through diet alone, but you can not be influenced by the Holy Spirit with a diet that is not geared toward veganism.

I would always recommend doing a proper cleansing before making a strict change in diet. In the Hebrew Israelite Community, we have a Sugarless Week and a Live Foods Week four times a year coinciding with the change in seasons. During these times we should do a proper, thorough cleaning out. We're a young collective community. We are in transition- learning, evolving and experiencing a life- moving from death to life. I went from eating animal by-products to veganism to, ultimately, live.

I've never had a problem disciplining myself from doing things if they aren't good for me. Over a year ago, I stayed in South Africa for a couple of months. I took internal cleansers and ate only fruits and vegetables- no sweets- sugar, honey or maple- no root vegetables and no soy. I drank fresh juices and almond milk sweetened with dates in the morning. I also took some herbs recommended by Dr. Sebi, a naturopathic healer practicing in Honduras. I ate one meal a day around 5:30 or 6:00pm, refraining from starchy foods. I did this for thirty days. As a result, I could run 5 to 7 miles with no problem. This became one of my greatest joys since adopting a live diet. I felt so good that I went beyond the 30 days to 9 months. During the Yom Kippur (Day of Atonement, See Leviticus 23: 26-32) I spent in South Africa, my mind was so clear and in harmony with nature that it was unbelievable. It was a joyous season. It allowed me to see the value of discipline. I'll never eat another way. This is the only way to eat.

139

KARYN CALABRESE - *Age 57*
Chicago, Illinois - **Raw for 25 years**

I am a walking testimony. I am 57 years old (with the body of a 25 year old). I have been vegan for 34 years and raw for 25. I haven't been sick in 30 years. I'm not aging. No wrinkles. No cellulite. My measurements are 34-21-34. Some people assume I'm too thin. I don't understand how one can be "too thin." I'm a dancer. I have danced at the University of Illinois with dancers in their twenties.

The women in my family died young. Now I have outlived all of them. My husband eats sixty-percent live and works at the restaurant with me. My children were raised vegan and my daughter currently eats about seventy-five percent live. I also have a grandson. I suffered from allergies and was sickly prior to my change in diet. I first learned about the live food diet when an airline hostess friend of mine told me about wheatgrass and the Ann Wigmore Clinic. Dr. Ann Wigmore was my teacher and inspiration. The rest is history.

"If you don't take care of this body where are you going to live?"

Over 100 patients have gone through our 30-day detox program at Karyn's. After the program they choose which direction they want to go with their diet. I have had a McDonald's executive with diabetes present a letter written by her doctor saying that the diabetes was gone. An 85 year old African American man who was advised to have his toe amputated from diabetes was completely healed. A woman who could barely walk was running up steps. One patient lost over 100 pounds. I've seen cancer patients with tumors reduced. A woman came in with 33 fibroids

and ended with 4. A medical doctor brought four of his patients to class. People are afraid to buck the system. After spending $20,000 on medical school and then learning that some $2 green juice can cure a disease is difficult to handle.

My advice? Detox. Detox. Detox. Detox. When going live, you will experience on-going healing crises. You should detoxify on a regular basis- 3 to 4 times a year. After the detoxification, it is the body's internal wisdom to naturally move to raw food. Find a mentor. Be careful of the person you are looking to for information. If it doesn't fit your belief system, let them go and find someone else. Find and establish a community of like-minded people because people are tribal. Don't be rigid with your diet; allow it to flow into your life. It's essential to have an open mind. If you come off as being a "know-it-all," who will listen? Also, you need a blender, juicer, food processor and dehydrator- a dehydrator just removes the moisture to prevent spoilage. It's not cooking. If you make it difficult on yourself, who will stay raw?

Changing one's diet puts a strain on relationships because so much is centered on food. None of my friends are raw, and due to my work schedule, I don't have a lot of friends. My best girlfriend does the detox program here and she's seventy-five percent raw. No one's invited me to Thanksgiving dinner in over 20 years. In past years, I didn't get invited out to dinner parties. I do now.

Going live reawakens your humanity to your fellow man. Any way one can be awakened is valid. People ask me what I had for breakfast and I tell them, "Prayer and meditation." I hope this dietary reawakening takes place all over the world. I tell people to take the button that says "NO WAR" and look in the mirror where it says "ON RAW." In ten years, I see myself doing the same as I am doing now, just doing it more and being more vibrant.

AMEN KHUM RA - *Age 35*
Washington, DC - **Raw for 5 years**

I was living the standard American life. I had a major health crisis related to my back and bladder. When you go through intense suffering, it causes you to break free from your previous form. Either I was going to be depressed and in misery or find a way to be happy. I found a way to change my consciousness and the principles of life. I learned that the first thing I have to do is cleanse my body temple. I decided I was going to do everything I could for my body to have the strength to heal itself.

David Wolfe inspired me with the message of eating life. I first met him at Everlasting Life Health Food Store when he was promoting his new book. At the time, I had spent 7 years as a vegan-starch-atarian; I was eating french fries each day. It was so clear and convincing that I gave up cooked food that day. I loss thirty pounds. I got immediate energy and a high. I felt lighter and there was a noticeable radiance in my skin. One of the challenges was dealing with family members who thought I was going to die because I was losing all the weight. I knew I would be okay because I was well-informed and had done so much reading. In about 3 months, I started gaining my weight back with no problem.

I have better bowel movements and haven't had a cold in 5 years. I used to have colds twice a year. It's a beautiful thing to enlighten others with your health by your presence. I used to take medication for allergies, I don't have them any more. I'm around people who have colds, but I don't catch them. I can tell there's no mucous in my body because a cold will try to come on, but it will go away. My sick leave at work is so large. The country would save so much on healthcare and man hours if everyone adopted the raw diet.

It's essential to have a juicer, blender and food processor. Some people need fancy dishes, but I don't have to have gourmet. I probably eat about 2 salads a day and fruit in the morning. Food today is not rich in minerals, so I take MSM (methylsulfonylmethane), spirulina, chlorophyll, and blue-green algae. I've gotten more into juicing and less into eating. It allows me to have more time, clarity and a purpose. You can really focus. You feel a lot of confidence. When you're eating cooked, you'll eat anything. With raw, it's the discipline of not just putting anything into your body.

Eat lots of greens to combat toxins. Start in a liquid form because you can't eat enough for what the body needs. Drink massive amounts- but one precaution. My wife learned that women have to watch how many greens they consume because it can make you constipated. She's 95% raw. Eat a lot of avocados and nuts to keep that "full" feeling. They were a lifesaver for me because jumping into just a fruit diet is hard. They also slow down the weight-loss. A lot of fiber creates a lot of gas. Gas is so harmful. It blocks oxygen from getting to cells. Consuming mostly juices, you hardly have any gas. To increase the hydrochloric acid in the stomach for proper digestion, juice a lot of celery.

My name means "The hidden mystical black life force." There's a life force energy in all living things. If you kill an animal, it's gone. With plants, it's still alive. When you pick it and eat it, it's still there. You are eating the purest form of sunlight. The whole purpose of being a spiritual being is to protect your life force energy. I found that diet and nutrition are the way to stay connected and raw food is at the height of it.

There's so much suffering in the world today, it becomes easier to embrace these "radical" ways of life. Ancient cultures often talk about the lotus. It's a beautiful flower that grows in muddy water. It teaches that out of the darkest circumstances comes the most beautiful transformation.

ANNETTE LARKINS *Age 62*
Miami, Florida - **Raw for 20 years**

When people see me and I tell them my age, they ask, "What are you doing? What's your secret? How do you stay so fit? So young?" It's surprising to them because so many of my peers are obese, diabetic, and overweight. It's more than just food or drink. It's fresh air and sunshine (although I don't need a tan). My blood pressure is that of a child. My family was plagued with diabetes and cancer, but I never had any of those things. Eating raw has created an all-around enhancement that has created a joy and happiness in me that I would not have been able to experience on a cooked diet. I have so much energy that if we could bottle it and sell it, I'd be a millionaire. My memory is enhanced and my waistline is smaller.

Raw food makes sense. In order to demonstrate the difference between life and death, I always use the carrot example. Try this at home. Cut the crowns from two carrots (about one inch thick); place one crown in a shallow dish of water. Before doing the same with the other one, subject it to a high heating process such as boiling, baking, frying, etc; then place both dishes on a window sill and watch what happens. When cooking food, you kill enzymes. If you eat living foods you are living.

When I first started what I call "The Kingdom of Living Foods," I had to find my way. I tried to sustain myself on salads and was bored stiff. My body said, "Oh no, girlfriend. You got put some zeal in this raw deal!" So I began to regroup. Now my diet consists of a variety of fruits, nuts, vegetables, seeds, and I do a lot of sprouting- buckwheat, sunflower greens, alfalfa, and cabbage. I drink wheatgrass and many other juices. I also dehydrate fruits and vegetables such as tomatoes and okra. When I became vegetarian in 1963, it was not for health reasons or religious beliefs. I simply began to abhor the taste, touch, and the smell of animal flesh. For years, I prepared two separate meals for my family because I thought it would be unfair to coerce them into my way of eating. My children who are now in their forties sometimes wish that I would have raised them vegetarian. If I had known then what I know now, I think I would have. My husband and I will soon celebrate our forty-third wedding anniversary. After all these years, he still treats me like a queen and highly respects the path that I have taken. In fact, he too wishes that he had taken it long ago. He knows that hospitals are filled with people who are digging their graves with their forks. He knows that I seldom complain of any ailments; and if I do, I know how to remedy them naturally.

Now I'm not speaking against the medical industry because it has its place. Nevertheless, we must take responsibility for educating ourselves so that we are better able to take care of ourselves. We should learn all we can about anatomy. Pay attention to yourself. How does your body react internally when you consume anything, or externally when you apply something? It is wise, although I didn't do it, to check with a holistic practitioner who is knowledgeable of the raw diet, especially if you are suffering from a disease.

Transition is the key. It's not advisable for most to make an abrupt change. You are not trying to win a race. Unless you are in dire need to do a drastic change, then do it at your own pace. You've got to deal with the psychology of it first. Don't deprive yourself. I gave up dairy products because they cause excess mucous, but I held on to cottage cheese because I knew that one day I would no longer desire it. Sometime later, I sprinkled cottage cheese on my salad like I normally did. I put a spoonful in my mouth and discovered that my taste buds were so sensitized that I tasted the carton the cheese came in. That was it for me.

I extend an invitation to you into the Kingdom of Living Foods to feast at the royal table of life, where you can drink in the beautiful sights and taste of the delicious cuisine. I hope that your experience will leave you enlightened and ready to enhance your existence through living foods. I bid you bon jour, bon voyage, and bon appetit!

THE TALIFERO FAMILY

STORM, 54, JINJEE, 37, SHALE, 3, JOME, 6, RAVEN,
10 ADAGIO, 6 months
Frazier Park, CA - **Raw for 6 months to over 30 years**

Jinjee: At the age of 26, I had chronic fatigue, hypoglyce-mia, a lump in my breast and I was overweight. I decided to dedicate my life to health. I met Storm two weeks later. When we met, he had been raw for over 20 years. He had a heart attack at 18 years old as a result of his bad diet. At 20, he became vegetarian on the pathway to 100% live. As Storm helped me change to raw foods, I went through a healing crisis. I had bad headaches, cold symptoms and shakes. I had fear because I was new to the diet and didn't understand what was happening. After Storm explained that my body was detoxifying, I just went through the process and it ended after 3 days.

There was a major difference in the ease of my labor during my pregnancies. I had Raven and Jome while I was eating cooked because, at the time, I didn't trust that the diet would form a healthy baby. By the time I had Shale and Adagio, I had more faith in the diet. My cooked pregnan-cies had labor that was 30 to 40 hours long, versus my raw pregnancies where my labor lasted 1 to 5 hours long. I did a lot of green juices, salads, and vegetables. None of our children have had any childhood illnesses, maybe one or two colds a year at the maximum and some haven't had any at all. I always had doubts with the kids to see if the diet was safe enough. I still get them tested for different things. I want to make sure that they are getting enough minerals if they look too skinny. I discovered the strangest thing- cel-ery does the best to put meat on their bones. Storm puts celery in his green juices to help him bulk up. He also consumes a lot of nut milks, avocados, olives, tons of citrus juice, apricots…he SWEARS by the protein in fruit.

Our diet is not extreme. We have balance with fruits, veg-etables, nuts and oil. It consists of 50% fruit: lots of orange juice, watermelon, mangoes, grapes, cherries, peaches,

plums, strawberries- whatever fruits are in season. One of our favorites is young coconuts. Twenty percent of our diet is vegetables in the form of salads, juices, green juices, vegetables in plain form (whole foods), salads placed in a blender, and Storm makes these wonderful herb salads with cilantro, parsley, avocados…Oh, and I love salsa and guacamole. We also eat nuts, sprouted grains, a few nut milks (soaked almonds, etc). We use condiments in our diet that many raw foodists shun like Celtic sea salt, raw honey, and cold-pressed olive oil. The diet of our children is pretty much the same, but they eat more fruit, a little less veg-etables- they love carrot and celery sticks, and eat a little more nuts. That's just what they prefer. We don't dehy-drate our food- maybe once or twice a month for fun to make special snacks for the kids, but that's all. When you dehydrate food, you're removing the water, which is kind of self-defeating. Water is essential to the diet.

What has helped us to stick with the diet is that the whole family is doing it. There's no temptation in our house. We home-school so our children don't get those outside influ-ences and we run our business from home so we don't have to worry about "power lunches" or ordering take-out. What also helps is living in nature. We're out in the boondocks. We don't have television so our children aren't bombarded with advertisements showing how much better your life can be if you eat junk. We do a lot of hiking, which keeps our connection with nature. There's a communion between nature and food. It helps you to be in a certain state of mind. Working in the area of raw food helps. Putting these thoughts into e-books, being able to help other people and seeing them use the information to help others gives you encouragement that this is a great diet and affects others positively.

When asked for advice about how to transition into the diet, I used to say transition slowly. First kick the dairy, coffee, etc. in the diet like I did. Go vegetarian for a while-a month to 6 months, then go vegan. Keep a rice and steamed vegetable dish so as not to shock the system. If you are in good health, you can go cold turkey. If you have a life-threatening condition where the doctors have written you off, then you should go on a fast at a fasting clinic where you can be monitored. Make 100% live your goal because you are so vibrant and alive that you can't even achieve that level if you are only 99%. Your pleasure in life comes from the feeling of health, not from the food.

MIGDAH BAHT ISRAEL - Age 33
Dimona, Israel - **Raw for 7 years**

According to our Spiritual Leader Ben Ammi, if you constantly consume toxic lies about eating, you will (if you haven't already) eventually become sick and completely miss the true pleasure of life with a living, vibrant soul. The mind/spirit and body/soul have to be fed on Truth. Truth about diet, health and living.* It's living foods that give you life more abundantly. You are what you eat. A profane spirit is fed on profane foods. Meat is profane. Processed foods are profane. They do not generate life because they do not feed the cells. They destroy them. Deviled foods (deviled eggs, deviled spam, etc.) is real because there is food for devils. These are foods that generate hatred and agitate the inner organs. Only the things that you do for Yah (God) will last. What's the point of eating live foods if your center is not the Creator? Your body was created to be a temple. I want my body to be a dwelling place for the Holy Spirit.

I first learned about raw food through Delights of the Garden raw food restaurant in Washington DC that used to be located near our health food store. A brother in our community encouraged me to eat there during one of our Raw Foods Weeks. At the restaurant, I saw someone eating something different and they let me taste it. I learned later that it was sea vegetables. I met brothers there who had a high level of consciousness. Shortly after that I traveled to our community in Israel. I went on a cleansing fast where I consumed nothing but grapes for 7 days. At the time I had an acute ear infection. The internal cleanse cleared it up, but this encouraged me to eat live food and to cleanse more frequently.

I eat 50% fruits, 40% vegetables, and 10% seeds and grains. I take flax seeds, sesame seeds, chlorophyll, and kelp. I would also take spirulina, but living overseas with the high cost, I haven't really had access to it in years. I used to have a sluggish digestive system. When I transitioned from meat-eating to vegan, there was a noticeable difference in my digestion; and when I ate live, it eliminated my need for artificial digestive aids. I also used to be anemic. I don't have any body odor so I don't use deodorant. My sense of smell, taste, and touch are much more sensitive. My mental clarity has improved. Live foods awaken your tastebuds. Being able to eat a watermelon without a coated tongue- to really taste it, has been my greatest joy.

Unfortunately, my teeth have been a challenge. Over the years, a slight shifting has taken place due to calcium and mineral deficiencies. That's not the fault of live foods. As a raw foodist, you have to have a high mineral intake. Live foods provide optimal nutrition, but with all things, if you fail to secure the proper food in its live state and you don't have variety, then you fall short of meeting your nutritional needs. You have to know what your needs are.

What's the point of eating live foods if your center is not the Creator?

I like the way live food makes me feel. I never wanted to go to the hospital. I never wanted to be sick. I haven't been sick since I have been on this diet, but I want to emphasize that it's not just the diet. It's the lifestyle. When you eat foods that promote healthy living, then you are propelled to seek knowledge that betters your life. Exercise, the way you eat, think, prayer and meditation, your environment are fundamental. As a vegan, it's important for me to see the difference in myself and in others because there was someone who initially told me about the diet and I had to see how they looked and performed. I keep thinking about those who are vegan, but not raw foodists in our community. They still maintain their youth and vitality because they apply Divine Law to their lifestyle and it has yielded the promised effects. They are my inspiration. I've seen our elders get better as they get older through consistency. They inspire me to stay consistent with my diet. If I can apply those principles to my life, then I can be like Sarah in the Bible who was 90 years old and FINE.

*Everlasting Life: from thought to reality by Ben Ammi (Communicators Press)

DR. ARIS LA THAM, Age 56
St. Mary's, Jamaica - **Raw for 28 years**

When I was younger, I had respiratory problems and a heart murmur. The change in diet has alleviated that. I first read about this diet from Dick Gregory, Ann Wigmore, Viktoras Kulvinskas. I've kept myself informed and took it on as a business. The best part about this is being in a position to help others and see their lives transform. Stanley Banks, George Benson's bass player, took one of my raw food workshops. He healed himself of an ulcer on his leg and went from 280-lbs to 190-lbs in a year. He's been featured on the cover of *Living Nutrition* (a raw food magazine).

I offer the following advice to those who are transitioning their diet from cooked to raw:

- Eat as much as you can raw and as frequently as necessary to be satisfied. If you ate one salad, eat another. It doesn't matter the food combination because they will be leveled out eventually. The food goes towards cleansing and repairing the cells in the body.

- A big challenge for others is that they can't find food, don't know what to eat, and so they revert back to cooked foods. I have learned to deal with that problem by consuming avocados, nuts (always soaked), sprouted grains, and dehydrated products.

- Be careful of the substitution mentality [Thinking of food in the context of "raw" lasagna or "live" burgers will cause the body to feel the effects as if you are eating cooked lasagna or burgers.]

- Taking vitamin supplements is totally unnecessary if you are eating all raw and drinking fresh vegetable and fruit juices

- For women who want to have a raw pregnancy, I recommend that they do live before they conceive. It's not good to change the diet while carrying the child because the cells will release toxins throughout the body. Eat green leafy vegetables and protein-rich foods. Drink juices and nut and seed milks. Breast-feed for 2 years and then introduce foods that are easily digestible to the baby.

- Seek support to have positive reinforcement.

- Cleanse the body.

- Keep reading and researching.

Did you know that Woody Harrelson, Demi Moore, Angela Bassett, Madonna, Sting, Lisa Bonet, Darryl Hannah, Donna Karan, and Sharon Stone are all raw foodists?

ARTIS EUGENE HINSON, Age 59
Greensboro, NC - **Raw for 32 years**

I plan to live to be at least 200 years old. Lee Chin Yeoung died at the age of 267 in 1933 as mentioned in Viktoras Kulvinskas' book Survival into the 21st Century. I believe that one could live forever in the raw lifestyle if it wasn't for the bad environment. I can still run, walk around my farm, ride bikes, climb trees and I hardly have any gray hairs. I'm seeking a higher reality and continue around all obstacles. My willpower is great. I'm moving toward the ultimate of existence.

I learned about the raw diet in the Essene Gospel of Peace by Edmond Szekely, Mucousless Diet Healing System by Arnold Ehret, and Dick Gregory's Cooking with Mother Nature. I reinforce my knowledge of the raw diet with the Bible and from what I've seen in other cultures. Most open-air markets sell mostly raw foods. Most of the world (except for affluent U.S. and European countries) ate live until the 1900s and after that a downward spiral occurred in the Western world. A book called Blatant Raw Food Fadist Propaganda by Joe Alexander talks about this. All the great teachers- Ghandi, Zoroaster, Muhammed, Jesus- were raw foodists. Einstein, Newton, Imenhotep, all the great philosophers were raw foodists.

I ate 85% raw for 22 years and 100% for the past 10 years. I fast 3 ½ days a week and eat 3 ½ days a week. I eat basically oranges- 225 a week. During tangerine season, I eat 300 tangerines a week. Sometimes, I eat my nori (seaweed) rolls and live pizza. I don't drink water. I haven't drunk water in 32 years because I get my water from my fruits and vegetables. I also supplement food with nuts- I just chew the nut and expel the pulp. I seldom get sick. Once in a while I get a "cold" – some call it a healing crisis- from chemicals in the environment. When I first started eating raw in 1973, I would get stomach aches and acid reflux as my body was adjusting to the diet. My bowels weren't easily moved. Now my bowels are 3 times a day on the raw diet. Even on a cooked vegan diet, they weren't regular.

I have more creativity and my love for my fellow humanity is much greater. I do, however, find it difficult to exist in relationships because I am looking for someone to go along with me. If they don't, then I can't relate. Another challenge for me is business. I run a natural food store- Body Ecology, prepare live foods, and make healing applications. Using my potions, I've healed people from all types of diseases that were considered "incurable"; and that includes AIDS, hepatitis, and cancer. I've made medicine for 45,000 to 65,000 people, which isn't a lot over 30 years. You would think that I would be rich by now, but it doesn't work that way. I constantly work for a living. One has to be accountable for their time here on earth or they will get retribution for their negativity.

Ten years ago, I bought 200 acres of land to build a spa in southern Virginia to start a natural community. The goal is for divine artists, healers, and teachers to come together to get rid of "incurable" ailments- I haven't seen anything incurable. I don't believe that hospitals have a place in this world. In a raw lifestyle, you won't even get into accidents because your sixth sense opens up to make you aware of impending danger. You won't have to worry about broken bones because the body doesn't lose calcium on uncooked foods.

Veganism promotes spirituality. Eating meat causes one to be grievous in their thoughts toward their fellow man. When God said, "Thou shall not kill," he didn't say, "except to eat." People have to evolve to where they are not seeking money, book knowledge, and physical things for this dietary revolution to take place. The Black man will be slow to get it until he is in economic parity with others. I see this raw movement happen more in affluent Black communities. If the whole world were raw, there probably wouldn't be any hunger. You've seen the statistics. There would be no water problems- it takes 25,000 gallons of water to produce 1-pound of beef. And we wouldn't be stupid enough to live in cold climates.

TOLENTIN CHAN - Age 43
New York, NY - **Raw for 6 years**

My family is really into eating during gatherings, so I had to open Quintessence Restaurant to get away! I love creating delicious meals for people who enjoy it so they will not miss their cooked foods. I believe that it is my calling to do this. When I eat cooked food, the whole feeling of my body isn't right.

I'm from Hong Kong and the Chinese cook everything because that's the theory of Chinese medicine. They believe that boiling makes everything more potent. The opposite is true with raw food. Since I was 6 years old, I've had asthma, I got sick all of the time, and my immune system was low. My parents tried everything- alternative surgery, acupuncture, Chinese herbs-nothing worked. I wasn't looking to cure my asthma by going raw, but it got cured.

I will never go back to eating cooked foods. To me it's suicidal. I won't do extreme things like some people, such as consuming all liquids. I'm always trying to balance my meals. I don't believe in the fruitarian diet because it's just fruit. Eat a variety of fruits and vegetables.

Eating raw is not the complete answer. I believe that everyone should do fasting. Your body is just like a house, you don't live in it for years without cleaning it. When I was researching enzymes, I came across a book called Live Food Recipes by David Jopp. I called him and set up a meeting. At the time, I had problems with my thyroid and I believe I had candida and lots of bloating. He put me on a 14-day fast. I felt so much better after the fast.

There are many who teach spirituality, but without the diet, it doesn't work. I tolerate stress more, I'm calmer, not as feisty- my family will attest to that- I'm more happy with myself, do yoga, and I'm reading spiritual books...years ago, I would never do that.

LYNDA CARTER - Age "over 50"
Richmond, VA - **Raw for 5 years**

Before becoming raw, my diet was like all other Black people-greasy. We fried everything. I was diabetic. I was beginning to lose my sight. My grandmother was diabetic and had both legs amputated. My mother died of a diabetic coma, and my godmother died of a stroke. Is that not inspiration enough?

Dr. Byron, a naturopathic doctor, first told me about the diet. I tried it. The third or fourth day, I felt like I had the flu. After that I was fine. It's been five years on July 17th. I feel better now than when I was 38; now I'm... over 50. It makes a difference. Living foods make me feel good and happy. They put life into my body. My attention span seems to be longer. I'm still overweight, but I lost 100 lbs.

Everything I eat is not organic because I can't get access to it. When people are adding on [including more raw food into their diets while still eating cooked food], they take things to supplement themselves. Greens, like kale, are a good superfood. I also eat MSM (methylsulfonylmethane), blue-green algae, and blueberries. I eat too many nuts.

Vegetarian is good; but to pick it up, go raw. A complete change occurs when changing from vegetarian to raw. When eating cooked, processed foods come into your diet. Even when you alter raw food, it's still living. Your vibe changes based on what you eat. People I come in contact with are not vicious. Each person has to do what he or she chooses. I've made up my mind that I'm not the food police. Some people will see me coming and run.

I love being able to share this with others and help them to heal. My son had asthma, ate raw for a month, and his health has improved. When I first started my business Alive and Raw, I didn't know anything about the food I make now. I made a raw cake for a 16 year old on live food. When her mother saw it, she cried.

DR LAILA O AFRIKA - Age 58
Ladies Island, SC - **Raw for 30 years**

I've been raw on and off for 30 years. I'm not bubbly about it; it's just what I do. When I started off, I didn't know any better. I didn't have any health issues. I thought that's what vegetarians were supposed to eat. We didn't use the terms "raw" or "live" foodist back then. I consume no cooked or processed foods. If you eat life, you stay alive. There's nothing to fear; fifty- to sixty-percent of the people on the planet eat raw/vegetarian food. The average American eats meat at least once a day. Even lions only eat meat once or twice a week. We are controlled by ignorance.

My greatest joy, however, is teaching children because they learn quickly and get into it when given the right information. My own son is 19 and my daughter is 29 years of age. What influence have I had on them? My daughter owns a vegetarian restaurant in Indianapolis and is in the process of opening up another. My son works for her. When they were little, we were eating eighty-percent raw. My daughter has been eating like this since she was twelve because she attended an African-centered school. My son was in public school, so he got contaminated. Today he eats veggie meat substitutes, Rice Dream and other junk foods made to taste like fast foods.

In the raw food movement, I don't see a large percentage changing as long as B.E.T. is on television. One of the problems of the movement is that we don't have the recruitment ability that McDonald's has. Recruitment is based on emotional appeal not information. I see that as a weakness in the Black community. The other health food movement crashed with Dr. Graham and Kellog in the '50s. Now we're left with "graham" crackers and "Kellog's" frosted flakes cereal. Junk food has invaded the health food stores. The meat and dairy industry won't give up that easily. Those who eat junk food eat what I call the "Willie Lynch" diet. We have to know who the enemy is- it's the people pushing the poor diet. My greatest challenge is getting Black people off white sugar. This has been an on-going struggle for 35 years and I'm losing.

I tell people to go slow because you have to do a lot of learning about food combining, nutrition, etc. Take one raw food meal a day so your taste buds can wake up again. Try not to make everything look and taste like junk food. By eating live, people have to know that what they are doing is intrinsically correct and they have to hold on. Know there's lots of support out there. They can e-mail me. I'll support them. llailaafrika@juno.com.

MSM
Methylsulfonylmethane is a sulfur that naturally occurs in organic food, but is destroyed when food is processed, heated, or dried. Good for hair, nails, and skin, MSM reduces allergy problems, aids in digestion, and strenghtens the immune system.

BILGAH BAHT ISRAEL, ELKAHYAM, SHLOMO, & AZEYAH BEN SHLOMO
Dimona, Israel - **Raw for 3 years**

I have been much more consistent with my children's diet than my own. My youngest child who is 3 ½ has virtually never eaten cooked food except for about six months of his life.

The benefits of eating all live versus cooked food have been quite apparent to me for some time now, but it was health problems that finally caused me to change our diet. I developed a horrible ulcer about three years ago that burned my insides night and day. Of more concern to me, my eldest son- Elkahyam who was always a chunky little boy began to waste away. He ate more than a normal child his age, but was getting skinnier. I had him tested for worms several times and although the results were negative most of the time I gave him worm treatment anyway. Until I finally realized that his body wasn't absorbing the nutrients from the food he was eating. So I changed his diet to a completely live diet- knowing that only live foods contained enzymes (life-giving activators that cause your body to be able to utilize the nutrients in food).

Within a very short time his condition dramatically improved. He gained weight and his appetite decreased. He ate less and gained more. It became apparent to me that his body had already evolved to a higher being that could not tolerate cooked enzyme-less foods. He thrives today physically being a very athletic and sharp child. When I was carrying Elkahyam I ate seventy- to eighty-percent fruit. Why? Because I was sick for the whole nine months and it seemed to be the only thing my body could keep down. He was born weighing nine pounds– at the time the biggest baby born in our birthing center. To this day, he prefers to eat fruit. I have to force him to eat his vegetables.

Now, my stomach ulcer didn't disappear as quickly. In the beginning of my live diet, I was eating a lot of soaked grains, especially buckwheat. I noticed that my stomach would always bother me shortly after my buckwheat salad. So I moved a step forward and took grains, oils, salt, and sugar completely out of my diet. Instant success! The day I stopped eating these foods was the day my stomach stopped bothering me. Nutritionally, I already knew these foods were acid-forming so I decided to cease any foods or habits that would contribute to the problem. I also observed that my complexion has dramatically improved and I have a lot more energy.

My baby boy Shlomo is nothing less than amazing. He'll eat almost any live food I give him. He loves fruit and raw vegetables. He'll eat raw cauliflower florets like it's a doughnut. My middle son Azeyah used to be ill a little more than my other two sons. I had the worst diet when I was carrying him. I ate a lot of cooked food and salt. He had terrible pus sores on his head. I tried everything, but nothing worked. When I changed his diet to all-live, "magic" happened again. His sores immediately improved and altogether disappeared. Need I say more?

I have also found that my children don't get sick at all. If they get a little down, it only lasts about 24 hours. I also clean them out regularly. Through trial and error, I have mastered what cooked foods I can cheat with and which ones give me an instant stomach ache. My primary objective is to never cheat and always eat all live because that's when I feel best. My children's discipline isn't much of a task. Their main problem is peer pressure.

ZACHARY RAMZEY III - Age 61
New Orleans, Lousiana - **Raw for 22 years**

I just came off a 15-day herbal fast ending with a 3-day water fast. I believe in fasting more than raw food. Eating is for children. As you get older, you will out-grow the need for a lot of gross matter. I haven't seen a high level of vibrant health in people who eat raw. The more you fast, the more you can refine your food intake when you return to eating. I fast every week. I've been doing it for so long, it's just a part of my life.

I've been a vegetarian for 35 years so live foods was the next logical step. I first learned of raw foods in the 70s from Dick Gregory and from a friend of mine in Chicago. I read Survival into the 21st Century and spoke with Viktoras Kulvinskas. I also learned from a brother named Walley Brooks who is a breathatarian who taught me to eat as light and as little as possible. When I do eat, my diet is exclusively organically-grown fruits and vegetables and herbal fasting regiments. I have never been sick or even had a cold in 35 years. I have reversed the aging process considerably to the extent that I am able to give an Egyptian Kemetic Yoga Session along with the healing Tao twice a day to young people who can't keep up. You have to return your body to an alkaline state.

At Detox International, we have a television and radio program and we are about to open up the largest wellness center in the country called the SynerG Complex. We have worked with hundreds of people. We feel there is no disease we can not turn around. We got into to this mess because we lost our will to live.

Everyone has to choose the right transitional period that's compatible with their spiritual mandate. I have met some wonderful people who eat meat and I've seen people I wouldn't associate with who eat raw. Divine spirituality is the key.

LILLIAN R BUTLER - Age 49
New York, New York - **Raw for 6 years**

I was vegetarian, but still experienced digestive problems and lack of energy. I was taking every kind of supplement imaginable. When a friend invited me to go to the Ann Wigmore Institute with her, I jumped at the opportunity. As a result, I'm happy to say that my poor digestion is much better, I have more energy, I stopped taking supplements and I do not have any health issues. I learned to eat things that take the least amount of energy to digest and gives me the most nutrition. When I returned home and told my husband I was eating this way, his response was, "Me, too."

When I first started, my diet was 2 ounces of fresh wheatgrass juice in the morning, and a salad with sprouts for lunch. At dinner, I ate whatever I wanted, be it cooked or raw. Now I eat a very simple diet most of the time. Salads, carrots, cucumbers, energy soup, juices. Since catering for our business Raw Soul, I eat more "sophisticated" raw meals: lasagna, pizza, veggie burgers, quiches and cakes.

When changing your diet to raw, I recommend going at a pace that is comfortable for you. Focus on nutrition rather than percentage of raw. Stay in tune to what your body needs. Relax and enjoy life. Make wheatgrass juice, leafy greens, fruit, and fermented foods a daily part of your diet; and you will still get there eventually. Decide how much raw you are going to eat each day. Plan your menus for the day. This way you know exactly what you are going to eat and are not swayed by whim. Don't be hard on yourself and stick with it. If your plan doesn't work out, make a new one. The success comes from the effort you put into it, not necessarily the end result. Perfection comes from being true to one's self and honoring one's body with what it needs. I DON'T believe that perfection means a 100% raw diet all the time. Being vegetarian does not necessarily mean that one is healthy. One could be vegetarian and eat fried foods, candy, cakes, ice cream, potato chips, and the like. It's all junk food!

KAHNUNAH BAHT ISRAEL
Dimona, Israel - **Raw for 11 years**

I had a health situation and wanted to see if live food would correct it. Over the years, my diet got better. I did it through discipline first, and second by being positive: knowing I can continue with it and be an example for those who want to be live.

I noticed changes with myself. My taste buds are more sensitive. What taste salty to me doesn't taste salty to others. My greatest joy has been creating new raw dishes. Most times they come out how I envision them in my mind. The hardest thing for me was giving up greens and cornbread. I loved greens and cornbread. Also stir-fries. I learned how to prepare them raw. Here in the desert, the sun is so hot that I can sun-bake food. I set it out on the hedges and cover it. I made some nut patties this way and they came out really good.

I don't consume sugar in my diet like that; if at all, it's maple syrup. I use spices like vegetable salt or sea salt to season my food. I don't consume tofu or soy products any more. I eat lots of nuts and flax seeds. The only oils I use are olive oil and sunflower oil, and I consume two tablespoons of flax seed oil daily. It keeps my digestive system open and it helps to burn fatty tissue with its Omega-3 fatty acids. I include noni juice, spirulina, barley, and alfalfa in my diet. These are blood purifiers.

I'm strong and healthy and had 3 babies who are strong and healthy. Three out of my five children were born on raw foods. While pregnant, I maintained the Sacred Diet- especially protein, cereals, raspberry tea, vitamins, and exercise. I'm very athletic. I was the first sister to go through our Expectant Mother Program. Twice a week we did callisthenic exercises and we see good results. My labors were shorter and I had almost painless births for my last two babies.

My children like live foods and eat live meals, but their diet is not 100% live. I haven't gone any further with the diet on my children because I have to be diligent. As an adult, sometimes I can go without. I have to make sure they have everything because their bones and teeth are developing.

Be sincere with changing your diet. Do it at a slow pace so the body doesn't go into shock. My pamphlet "All the Way Live" has simple menus to wean you off cooked food.

I feel real good and still have all of my teeth. I'm really only 33 years old. Really.

"I have been eating 95% to 100% live for many years because of my own personal zeal. I believe that a doctor has to set the pace for everyone else and be an example of health for the community. In the present society, medical doctors can be overweight and smoke and still be considered doctors."
- Dr. Ahmadiyah Ben Israel, Divine Ministry of Health, Hebrew Israelites of Jerusalem

---

DICK GREGORY, Age 73
Plymouth, MA - **Raw for 37 years**

We've got to stop talking about dying with dignity and talk about living with dignity. Once you do that, your whole chemistry changes- especially fear.

I became vegetarian in 1963 and progressed from there. I didn't do it for health reasons- I still drank alcohol and smoked cigarettes back then. The Civil Rights Movement inspired me. A Mississippi sheriff kicked my pregnant wife and it didn't make sense to watch him kick her without killing him, but I killed animals to eat them. Non-violence means nothing should be killed. I didn't know animal products were bad because the Klu Klux Klan didn't give them to me; people who loved me did. I never thought my mother or the church would give me something that was bad for me. For me, good nutrition was when you had food to eat and bad nutrition was when you didn't have anything.

Before I changed my diet, my weight never went over 155 pounds. I suffered from sinus trouble and ulcers so bad they had me crawling on the floor. Dr. Alvina Fulton, a great nutritionist- taught me how to fast and the benefits of raw food. After becoming vegetarian, I actually gained weight. My sinuses and ulcers cleared up. Now I figured if my condition could improve while I was still smoking and drinking, then there had to be something to this.

I had to save my life and the lives of others. I raised 10 children on raw food. Eighty-percent of their diet was fruit. It wasn't hard because my wife couldn't cook. She'd burn kool-aid. Most of what children eat is what you eat. The only problem is at school. Now my concern was how do I get this information to others? If I am sitting on T.V. saying this and that about nutrition, but a white Harvard nutritionist is sitting next to me [saying the opposite], my own grandmother would believe the white Harvard nutritionist. So I decided to pull a stunt. In 1976, I created the Dick Gregory Bicentennial Run to Dramatize World and Domestic Hunger. I ran 50 miles a day from New York to Los Angeles for 71 days consuming nothing but liquid, no solids. I did it for the love of my people so I could tell the white Harvard nutritionist to shut up!

I did my first liquid fast in 1967 against the war in Vietnam. I've also done a 40-day water fast. The longest I have fasted on water was 82 days. My longest air fast was 8 days- I was going for 12, but I had to travel. An air fast means to abstain from *everything*. It's a serious fast and you can't do anything while you are on it. The more you do it, the more you get used to it. I've done it 20 times. I believe people should be breathatarians because when you think about it, eating is a violation. Some say check with your doctor first, but do you check with your doctor when you smoke cigarettes and drink alcohol? I can't check with my doctor because he's dead.

I don't believe that there is a connection between spirituality and vegetarianism. I've seen people eat the butt out of a pig with more spirituality than some vegans I know. I do, however, believe that you can become more spiritual through changes in diet. But I'll tell you what the top 3 killers are: sleep deprivation, dehydration, and lack of physical fitness. We have so much misinformation. We've been given a false image of health and have been led to believe that someone is healthy because they "look healthy." What is it about Muslims who don't drink, smoke, or do drugs when they live in the midst of people who do? Why hasn't anyone studied them?

This Winter Solstice, I'm announcing that I'm eating all fruit until we get a federal law to end police brutality, until veterans get treated right in the U.S., until the FBI and CIA are done away with, and until Homeland Security is totally done away with and replaced with something that does not violate human rights. The fast will bring attention to these issues- maybe it won't last long, or maybe I'll be doing it for the rest of my life. What inspires me? Blacks are 12% of the American population, but 87% of those on dialysis, 83% of the prison population, and 98% of women with fibroids are Black women. The type of cancer I was diagnosed with in the '90s is one of the rarest forms and only people who work with nuclear materials get it. Since I have not been working around nuclear materials, it's no mystery I got it. When I went back this year to get examined, they told me that they saw no traces of the cancer anywhere in my body.

Recommended Readings for Body, Mind & Spirit

Survival In to the 21st Century by Viktoras Kulvinskas
A source of inspiration for many long-term raw foodists.

Nature's First Law by Arlin, Dini, & Wolfe
Great beginners guide for understanding why "cooked food is poison."

Afrikan Holistic Health by Dr. Llaila O. Afrika
Lots of great information on the history of the medical industry and precautions that should be taken by people of African descent.

Prescription for Nutritional Healing by Phyllis A. Balch & James F. Balch, M.D.
Reference guide for naturally alleviating sickness and disease. (We do not endorse the non-vegan treatments.)

Conscious Eating by Gabriel Cousens
A wonderful new way to enjoy your food.

Juice Fasting and Detoxification by Steve Meyerowitz
A great book showing how to fast for heatlh and longevity.

Fast Food Nation by Eric Schlosser
How mega-corporations have destroyed the health of the people.

God the Black Man and Truth by Ben Ammi
Raises one's consciousness about how the world has been deceived on every level of existence.

The Master Key System by Charles F Hannell
A practical guide on how to elevate the process of thought.

The Alchemist by Paulo Coehlo
A cute, yet powerful story about the power of thought.

The Scofield Reference Bible (KJV) (1967) edited by C.I. Scofield.
The most well-researched and closest translation to the original Hebrew text. Where the New Testament contradicts the Old Testament, we go with the Old.

Last Hours of Ancient Sunlight by Thom Hartmann
An update on the state of the planet and why we will no longer exist if we don't take action.

Additional Resources

RAW FOOD RESTAURANTS

Everlasting Life Health Food Store
2928 Georgia Avenue NW
Washington DC 20001
(202) 232-1700

Everlasting Life Health Complex
Hampton Mall/ Kingdom Square
9185 Central Avenue, Capital Heights MD
20743. Phone: (301) 324-6900
www.everlastinglife.net

Everlasting Life Raw
878 Ralph David Abernathy Blvd, Atlanta
GA 30317. Phone: (404) 758-1110

Karyn's Fresh Corner & Inner Beauty Ctr
1901 North Halsted Street, Chicago, IL
60614. Phone: (312) 255-1592
www.karynraw.com

Quintessence raw food restaurant- 3 locations in New York.
566 Amsterdam Avenue (Between 87th &
88th St.) New York, NY 10024. Phone: (212)
501-9700
www.quintessencerestaurant.com

Alive & Raw catering to MD, DC & VA
Phone: (804) 863-0635
www.aliveandraw.com

Raw Soul take-out, catering, and potlucks
745 St. Nicholas Avenue
New York NY 10031
Phone: (212) 875-7112
www.rawsoul.com

Arnold's Way
319 W Main Street
Store #4 Rear
Lansdale PA 19446
(215) 361-0116
www.arnoldsway.com

Sunshine & AJ
747 4th Street, Miami FL 33139
(305) 674-9960
www.foodwithoutfire.com

HOLISTIC HEALING INSTITUTIONS

Everlasting Life Health Clinic
1433/1 Sederot Aliyah
Dimona, Israel 86000
www.kingdomofyah.com

Dr. Sebi
Known for curing "incurable" diseases
including AIDS. Also located in Los Angeles,
CA; and has a healing village in Honduras.
12908 SW 132 Court, Miami, FL 33186,
(305) 252-1800
www.drsebi.com

Queen Afua
Author of Heal Thyself & Sacred Woman
106 Kingston Ave
Brooklyn NY 11213
718-221-HEAL (4325)
www.queenafuaonline.com

Detox International in New Orleans, Louisiana teaches African-Americans how to heal.
Lake Forest Plaza
5700 Read Boulevard, Suite 710
New Orleans LA 70127-8400
(504) 304-0070
www.detoxinternational.com,
www.thesynergcomplex.com

Dandelion Bunch is a support and community service group in Philadelphia, PA with a focus on African-Americans
(215) 849-0181
Website: www.dandelionbunch.com
E-mail: dandelionbunch@aol.com

Ann Wigmore Institute
PO Box 429
Rincón, Puerto Rico 00677
(787) 868-6307 or (787) 868-0591
Website: www.annwigmore.org

Body Ecology
926 Stephens St.
Greensboro, NC 27406
(336) 273-7406
www.bodyecol.net

WEBSITES

Raw Soul Chat Group

Raw (Live) food support group with a focus on people of African descent
http://groups.yahoo.com/group/RawSoul/

Living and Raw Foods website- an enormous wealth of resources and information
www.rawfoods.com

Annette Larkins has books and a syndicated health show based in Miami, Florida.
www.annettelarkins.com

The Meatrix.com: A hilarious and informative cartoon about the meat industry.
www.themeatrix.com

RAW FOOD RETREATS

VegSoul hosts retreats in Jamaica.
Phone: 1-888-VEG-SOUL (834-7685)
Website: www.vegsoul.com

International Raw and Living Foods Festival held each year in Portland, Oregon
Website: www.rawfood.com

The Talifero Family
Offers retreats in California
E-mail: info@thegardendiet.com
Website: www.thegardendiet.com

RAW FOOD PUBLICATIONS

Living Nutrition Magazine
www.livingnutrition.com

Just Eat An Apple
www.justeatanapple.com

Order Form

To order additional copies of <u>The Joy of Living Live: A Raw Food Journey</u>:

Telephone: (202) 797-8110

Website: www.kingdomofyah.com/cponline

Postal Mail: Communicators Press, P.O. Box 26063, Washington DC 20001

Please send me ___ **copies**

Name: _____

Address: _____

_____

Phone: _____

E-mail: _____

Price: $19.95 per copy plus $5.00 shipping and handling (add $0.75 for each additional copy. We accept checks, money orders, credit cards, and debit cards.

Amount enclosed: _____

We want to hear from you! Please send all questions, comments, and suggestions to the mailing address above or e-mail: *thejoyoflivinglive@yahoo.com*

Thank you for your order!

Zakhah

Order Form

To order additional copies of The Joy of Living Live: A Raw Food Journey:

Telephone: (202) 797-8110

Website: www.kingdomofyah.com/cponline

Postal Mail: Communicators Press, P.O. Box 26063, Washington DC 20001

Please send me ___ copies

Name: _____

Address: _____

_____

Phone: _____

E-mail: _____

Price: $19.95 per copy plus $5.00 shipping and handling (add $0.75 for each additional copy. We accept checks, money orders, credit cards, and debit cards.

Amount enclosed: _____

We want to hear from you! Please send all questions, comments, and suggestions to the mailing address above or e-mail: *thejoyoflivinglive@yahoo.com*

Thank you for your order!